500 Metal Vessels

Books are to be returned on or before
the last date below.

500 Metal Vessels

CONTEMPORARY EXPLORATIONS OF CONTAINMENT

LARK BOOKS

A Division of Sterling Publishing Co., Inc.

New York / London

Editor: **Marthe Le Van**
Art Director: **Kathleen Holmes**
Cover Designer: **Cindy LaBreacht**
Assistant Editors: **Cassie Moore, Mark Bloom**
Associate Art Director: **Shannon Yokeley**
Art Production Assistant: **Jeff Hamilton**
Editorial Assistance: **Dawn Dillingham**
Art Intern: **Michael Foreman**
Proofreader: **Jessica Boing**

Cover
David Bausman, *Airavata,* 2006

Spine
Christopher A. Hentz, Untitled, 1998

Back cover, top left
Hanjoo Kim, *Pill Container for Respect,* 2005

Back cover, top right
Elliott Pujol, *Tuscan Vessel,* 1996

Back cover, bottom left
David A. Huang, *Luminous Relic #496,* 2006

Back cover, bottom right
Felicity Peters, *Loving Cups,* 2000

Front flap
(Top) Helen Shirk, *Clarice's Fancy,* 2004
(Bottom) Nicole Jacquard, *Dahlia Bud Vase,* 2000

Back flap
Dong Hyun Kim, *Untitled Vessel,* 2006

Title page
Helen Shirk, *Commemorative Cup,* 2000

Opposite
(Left) Pamela Morris Thomford, *Valiant Duty (Tzdekah/Alms Box),* 2004
(Right) Dennis Nahabetian, *Spring Lotus,* 2006

Library of Congress Cataloging-in-Publication Data

500 metal vessels : contemporary explorations
of containment / editor, Marthe Le Van.—1st ed.
   p. cm.
   Includes index.
   ISBN-13: 978-1-57990-876-8 (pb-with flaps : alk. paper)
   ISBN-10: 1-57990-876-4 (pb-with flaps : alk. paper)
   1. Metal containers—History—21st century.
I. Le Van, Marthe.   II. Title: Five hundred metal vessels.
NK8459.C65A17 2007
739—dc22
                        2007013614

10 9 8 7 6 5 4 3 2 1

First Edition

Published by Lark Books, A Division of Sterling Publishing Co., Inc.,
387 Park Avenue South, New York, N.Y. 10016

Text © 2007, Lark Books
Photography © 2007 Artist/Photographer as noted

Distributed in Canada by Sterling Publishing,
c/o Canadian Manda Group, 165 Dufferin Street
Toronto, Ontario, Canada M6K 3H6

Distributed in the United Kingdom by GMC Distribution Services,
Castle Place, 166 High Street, Lewes, East Sussex, England BN7 1XU

Distributed in Australia by Capricorn Link (Australia) Pty Ltd., P.O.
Box 704, Windsor, NSW 2756 Australia

If you have questions or comments about this book, please contact:
Lark Books
67 Broadway
Asheville, NC 28801
(828) 253-0467

Manufactured in China

ISBN 13: 978-1-57990-876-8
ISBN 10: 1-57990-876-4

**For information about custom editions, special sales, premium and
corporate purchases, please contact Sterling Special Sales
Department at 800-805-5489** or specialsales@sterlingpub.com.

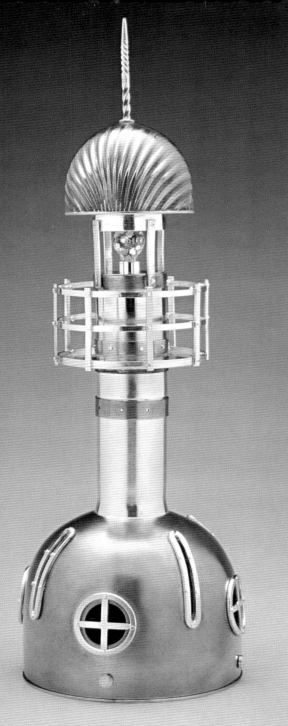

Contents

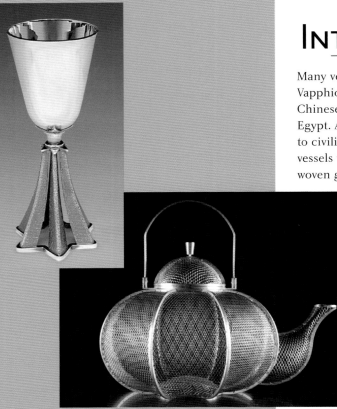

INTRODUCTION

Many vessels have become famous—the Holy Grail, the Vapphio cups and containers of Greece, the wonderful Chinese celadon vases, the tall stone forms of ancient Egypt. All are iconic examples that have greatly contributed to civilization's development and sense of aesthetics. Early vessels were made of wood, stone, leather, large leaf forms, woven grasses, clay, and metal. These vessels were used for food preparation, presentation, and storage; for ceremonial and religious purposes; for celebratory and cultural functions such as marriage, betrothal, birth, death, and all the rites and functions that constitute the human experience.

For centuries, collectors have vied with one another in their zeal to own snuff and tobacco boxes, perfume containers, pillboxes, chatelaines, liquor flasks, matchboxes, and sewing kits. The design of such archetypal vessels continues to evolve through the inspired minds and skillful hands of modern metal artists. John E. Cogswell's *Kiddush Cup*, a Jewish ceremonial vessel, is masterfully conceived and handwrought (left, top). Many works are visionary expressions of the teapot form, such as David Bausman's *Airavata* (page 401) and Dong Hyun Kim's Untitled Vessel (page 82).

Many of the works included in this collection challenge our assumptions of what a vessel "should be." Soon Chan Hwang (left, bottom), Sung-Yeoul Lee (left, center), and Dennis Nahabetian (page 183) work with mesh to construct vessels that are breathtaking to behold. In *The Tower of the Dreams* (page 29), Alexandru Usineviciu

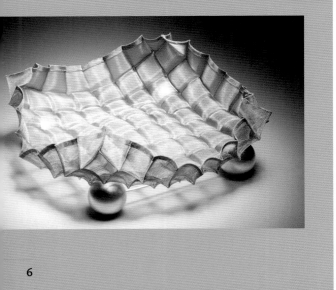

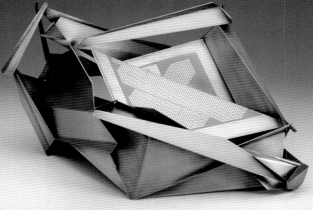

achieves a similar feat with spiraled and interlinked brass wire. In these pieces, sculptural qualities take precedence over conventional function. They challenge the perceptions of the viewer and act as a stimulus for thought. Other such transcendent vessels include *Endgame* by Ron Hinton (right, top), *Luminous Relic #496* by David A. Huang (right, center), and *Formal Transgression #2* by Daniel Randall (page 191). Objects of beauty and contemplation can be considered functional, but not in a literal way. They serve a different purpose—to stir the mind, the soul, and the senses.

As you observe this collection, you will see that metal art is a particularly dynamic and thriving media. Artists around the globe are making original forms, often using new materials in an innovative and creative manner reflecting our times. In Yeonkyung Kim's *Step by Step* (page 376) and Ju-Wen Hsiao's *Bowl. Cup-a, Bowl. Cup-b* (page 377), the notion of the collapsible vessel is imaginatively articulated and superbly engineered. Contemporary social concerns of sustainability and consumption are cleverly presented in Susan Myers's *Disposable Series* (right, bottom) and Miel-Margarita Paredes's *Turkey Walker* (page 358).

The work of the artist is to interpret, preserve, inspire, and alter our perceptions. It is to create a dialogue between function, use of material, concept, and imagination. Above all, it is to make us think, to make us feel. To that end, I hope that these *500 Metal Vessels* provide a stimulating and expressive experience for the viewing audience.

Fred Fenster

Page 6, from top: John E. Cogswell, *Kiddush Cup,* 2006; **Sung-Yeoul Lee,** *Teapot in Meshed Form,* 2006; **Soon Chan Hwang,** *Embossed,* 2005

Page 7, from top: Ron Hinton, *Endgame,* 1998; **David A. Huang,** *Luminous Relic #496,* 2006; **Susan Myers,** *Disposable: Chinese Takeout,* 2003–2005

Kristie Reiser
Beginning | 2005

EACH, 10½ X 3 X 3 INCHES (26.7 X 7.6 X 7.6 CM)
Pewter; raised, cast, fabricated
PHOTO BY BILL LEMKE

Sun Kyoung Kim

Palace | 2001

FROM LEFT, 3½ X 3 X 2 INCHES (8.9 X 7.6 X 5.1 CM)
5 X 2½ X 2½ INCHES (12.7 X 6.4 X 6.4 CM)
8 X 8 X 4 INCHES (20.3 X 20.3 X 10.2 CM)

Copper, silver plating; fabricated

PHOTO BY ARTIST

Suzanne Amendolara

Above the Water | 2006

3 X 6 X 3 INCHES (7.6 X 15.2 X 7.6 CM)

Sterling silver, 18-karat gold; formed, fabricated

PHOTO BY ARTIST

Alberto Zorzi

Vase | 2005

11¾ X 4 X 11¾ INCHES (30 X 10.2 X 30 CM)

Sterling silver

PHOTO BY F. COPPITZ
COURTESY OF PAMPALONI GALLERY, FLORENCE, ITALY

John B. Gilliam
Ibex Goblet | 1999
7 X 3 X 3 INCHES (17.8 X 7.6 X 7.6 CM)
Sterling silver; raised, spun, soldered
PHOTO BY PETER GROSEBECK

John E. Cogswell

Elijah's Cup | 1993

13 X 6 INCHES (33 X 15.2 CM)

Sterling silver; raised,
fabricated, handwrought

PHOTO BY ARTIST
COURTESY OF THE JEWISH MUSEUM,
NEW YORK, NEW YORK

Robin Kraft

New Crop II | 2005

8 X 8 X 5 INCHES (20.3 X 20.3 X 12.7 CM)

Sterling silver, fine silver, enamel, stainless steel, patina;
die formed, fabricated, cast

PHOTO BY DEAN JOHNSON

Anne Hallam

Memory | 2002

9½ X 8½ X 6 INCHES (24.1 X 21.6 X 15.2 CM)

Sterling silver; fabricated

PHOTO BY ARTIST

Lin Stanionis

Flores de la Lengua | 2002

6 X 5 X 3 INCHES (15.2 X 12.7 X 7.6 CM)

Bronze, wax, polymer clay; cast

PHOTO BY JON BLUMB

Barbara Minor
Untitled | 2004

4 X 6 X 6 INCHES (10.2 X 15.2 X 15.2 CM)

Glass, enamel, fine silver, 24-karat gold foil, copper, sterling
silver, onyx, carnelian, bone; raised, fabricated

PHOTOS BY RALPH GABRINER

Helen Shirk

Curved Pod | 2002

18 X 11 X 7 INCHES (45.7 X 27.9 X 17.8 CM)

Copper, patina, colored pencil

PHOTO BY ARTIST

David Griffin

Under One Roof | 2006

18 X 6 X 6 INCHES (45.7 X 15.2 X 15.2 CM)

Copper, sterling silver, spalted maple, gold leaf, rock, patina; constructed, fabricated, spun, turned, powder coated

PHOTO BY ARTIST

Momoko Okada

Moon Incense Burner | 2006

8 X 8 X 8 INCHES (20.3 X 20.3 X 20.3 CM)

Brass, silver, shakudo; damascened, raised, spun, inlaid

PHOTO BY SHINANO

Mark Herndon

Space Vessel #3 | 2003

4 X 3 X 3 INCHES (10.2 X 7.6 X 7.6 CM)

Damascus steel, brass

PHOTOS BY ARTIST

Ron Hinton

Endgame | 1998

11 X 16 X 20 INCHES (27.9 X 40.6 X 50.8 CM)

Bronze, copper; computer-generated drawing,
photoetched, formed, fabricated

PHOTO BY JON BLUMB

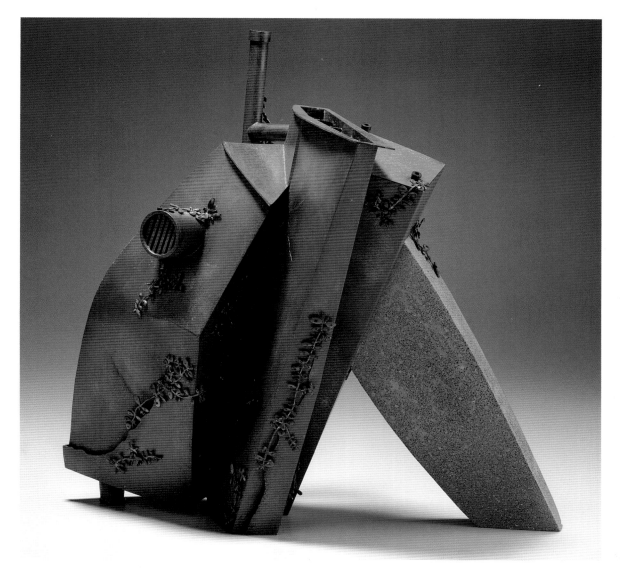

Amy Bailey

Breakage and Exposure (Teapot) | 2003

13 X 12½ X 6½ INCHES (33 X 31.8 X 16.5 CM)

Copper, enamel, cement, porcelain seeds; fabricated

PHOTO BY M. LEE FATHERREE

Patricia A. Nelson

Dicranurus Monstrosus The Magnificent | 2001

12 X 14 X 14 INCHES (30.5 X 35.6 X 35.6 CM)

Copper, trilobite fossil, ebonized oak; raised, etched, forged, constructed

PHOTO BY SERENA NANCARROW

John J. Rais

Hard Leisure | 2005

24 X 29 X 20 INCHES (61 X 73.7 X 50.8 CM)

Steel, copper, paint, patina; forged

PHOTO BY D. JAMES DEE

The vase, unlike some other functional vessels, provides an opportunity for artistic collaboration with others, and that is a great part of its appeal to me. It is inherently not just my single artistic expression. As the vase is used by others to create new artistic compositions through the addition of natural plant materials, it will always be part of an ongoing improvisational design process. —TO

Tom Odell

Vase | 1999

21¼ X 10½ X 10 INCHES (54 X 26.7 X 25.4 CM)

Bronze, patina; lost wax cast

PHOTO BY DEAN POWELL

These vessels are examples of how an artist can take an industrial process and create unique objects that speak of something beyond process. I have been working on the lathe for 30 years and still have new ideas to pursue. —LH

Lynne Hull

Black-N-White Vases | 2005

EACH, 14 X 7 X 5 INCHES (35.6 X 17.8 X 12.7 CM)

Copper, paint; spun, fabricated, sanded

PHOTO BY HAP SAKWA

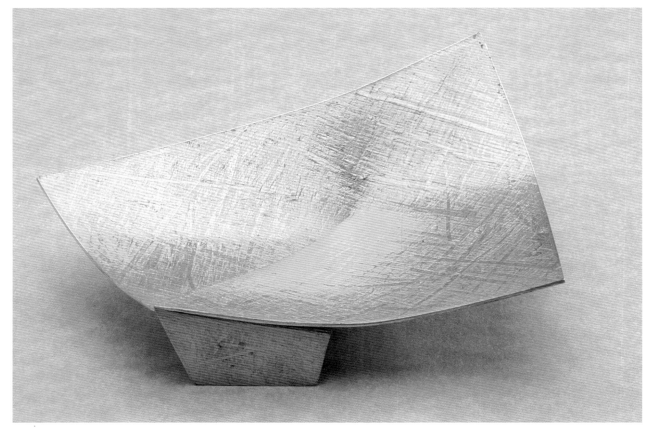

Felicity Peters

Bowl: Vessel for Fragile Dreams—Life's Fabric | 2000

4½ X 5 X 4 INCHES (11.4 X 12.7 X 10.2 CM)

Sterling silver, 24-karat gold; folded, constructed, kum boo

PHOTO BY VICTOR FRANCE

Alexandru Usineviciu
The Tower of the Dreams | 2004
20 X 8 X 8 INCHES (50.8 X 20.3 X 20.3 CM)
Brass wire; spiraled, interlinked
PHOTO BY ARTIST

The gold foil is functional as well as beautiful.
It protects the flavor of the tea. —LSK

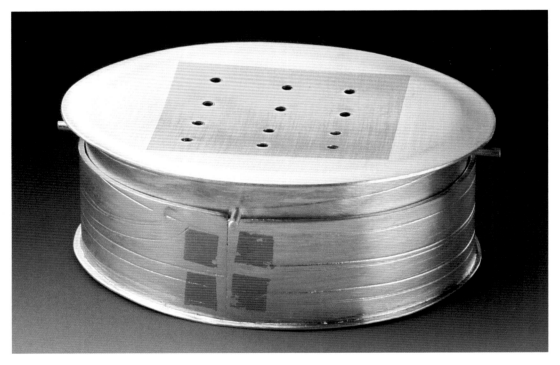

Lanie S. Kodner
Zen Tea Caddy | 2006

1 X 1¾ X 2¼ INCHES (2.5 X 4.4 X 5.7 CM)

Fine silver, sterling silver, 24-karat yellow gold foil; hand
fabricated, roll printed, kum boo

PHOTO BY DON CASPER

Felicity Peters

Loving Cups | 2000

LARGEST, 3¼ X 1¾ X 1¾ INCHES (8.3 X 4.4 X 4.4 CM)

Sterling silver, 24-karat gold; hand raised, kum boo

PHOTO BY VICTOR FRANCE

Darlys Ewoldt

Nexus of Memories II | 2005

8 X 23 X 21 INCHES (20.3 X 58.4 X 53.3 CM)

Copper, patina; angle raised, formed, fabricated

PHOTO BY ARTIST

Gregory Lavoie

Pod | 2004

6 X 4 X 4 INCHES (15.2 X 10.2 X 10.2 CM)

Copper, brass; fold formed, constructed

PHOTO BY ARTIST

Jean Mandeberg

Reliable Confections | 2005

6 X 17 X 16 INCHES (15.2 X 43.2 X 40.6 CM)

Tin museum tags, steel tacks, wood

PHOTOS BY MICHAEL RYAN

Boris Bally

"P" Is for Platter | 2003

30¹/₈ X 30¹/₈ X 3 INCHES (76.5 X 76.5 X 7.6 CM)

Recycled aluminum traffic signs, recycled deckplate, scrap aluminum, copper; hand spun, hand fabricated, pierced, cold joined, buckshot planished

PHOTO BY DEAN POWELL

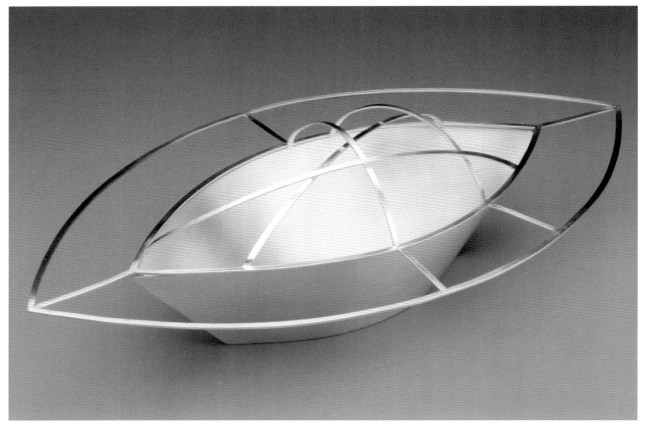

Sujin Lim

Vase | 2002

4 X 13½ X 7½ INCHES (10.2 X 34.3 X 19 CM)

Sterling silver; soldered, formed

PHOTO BY MICHAEL CAVANAGH AND KEVIN MONTAGUE

Monica Schmid
Apple Bowls | 2000

3½ X 8 X 3½ INCHES (8.9 X 20.3 X 8.9 CM)
Silver; etched, fabricated, raised, cast, carved
PHOTO BY THE IMAGERY GROUP

I draw my tableware subjects directly from the gut, in a manner of speaking. Growing up in a culture where mothers measured the health of their children by the size of their rosy cheeks, I watched my mother prepare gigantic bowls of applesauce for our large family in Switzerland. I remember being fascinated by the perfect spirals of the apple peel left on the newspaper, and that memory inspired my creation of the bowls. —MS

Jason THE YORK

Untitled | 2005

10 X 4 X 5 INCHES (25.4 X 10.2 X 12.7 CM)

Sterling silver, wood; raised, formed, soldered, planished, filed, sanded, polished, carved

PHOTO BY ENSLEY PHOTOGRAPHY

Elizabeth Ditter
Two Become One | 2005
6 X 4 X 10 INCHES (15.2 X 10.2 X 25.4 CM)
Sterling silver, wood, rubber O rings
PHOTOS BY ROBLY GLOVER

Ann L. Lumsden

Hinged Vases | 2000

3¼ X 5½ X ⅝ INCH (8.3 X 14 X 1.6 CM)

Sterling silver, glass test tubes; cast, hand fabricated

PHOTO BY ARTIST

Michael B. Hays

Bud Vase | 2005

5½ X 1½ X 1¾ INCHES (14 X 3.8 X 4.4 CM)

Sterling silver, rubber, glass; fabricated

PHOTO BY CHAS KRIDER

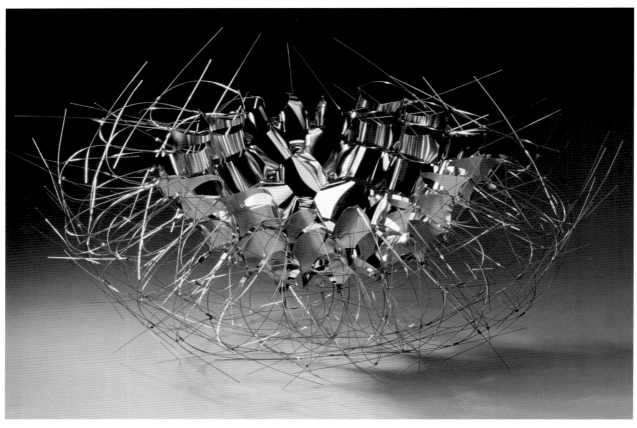

Nathan Poglein

Converge | 2006

12 X 22 X 22 INCHES (30.5 X 55.9 X 55.9 CM)

Stainless steel

PHOTOS BY JEFF SABO

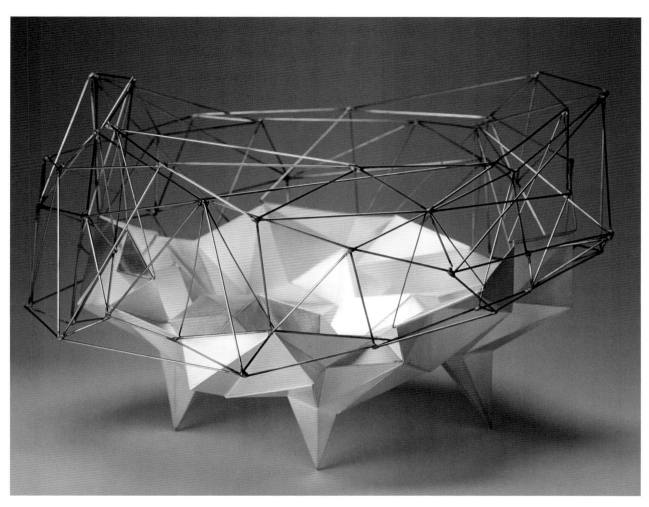

Wook Koh

Tornado | 2003

9 X 13 X 12½ INCHES (22.9 X 33 X 31.8 CM)
Sterling silver, stainless steel; scored
PHOTO BY MUNCH STUDIO

Elliott Pujol

Light Gather | 1981

7 X 13 INCHES (17.8 X 33 CM)

Bronze

PHOTO BY ED STURR

June Schwarcz

#2298 | 2006

11½ X 6 INCHES (29.2 X 15.2 CM)

Copper screening, black patina; electroplated

PHOTOS BY M. LEE FATHERREE

Dianne Frank

Grace, Grace, and Grace | 2006

16¼ X 13 X 14 INCHES (41.3 X 33 X 35.6 CM)

Copper, nickel

PHOTO BY DAVID GRIFFIN

Michael J. Parrett

Stuck in the Middle | 2006

12 X 3 X 4 INCHES (30.5 X 7.6 X 10.2 CM)

Copper, gesso, prismacolor, oil paint, heat patina; fabricated

PHOTO BY ARTIST

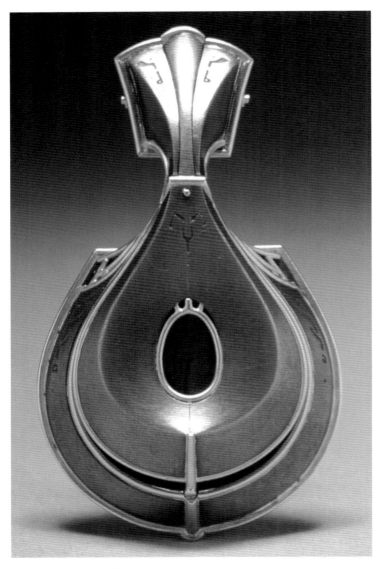

Seeds are beautiful for the growth, possibility, and promise that they embody. In my work, they symbolize not only the natural world, which deserves our respect and safekeeping, but also the finest potential of human nature. The purpose of my vessels is to shelter and protect, yet they are also made to be handled and experienced. The seeds are held securely but can be glimpsed through openings in the exterior. I believe in the necessity and value of this shared interaction. If one leaves openings, suggesting an invitation, others will be compelled to accept the offering, to investigate and to discover. —CC

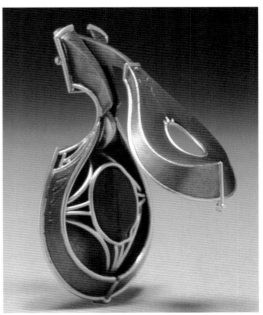

Cappy Counard
What We Hold | 2005

2½ X 1⅜ X ⅜ INCH (6.4 X 3.5 X 0.95 CM)

18-karat gold, copper, wisteria seed; scored, folded, fabricated

PHOTOS BY ARTIST

Mark Nelson

Ceremonial Bowl | 1996

4 X 4 X 4 INCHES (10.2 X 10.2 X 10.2 CM)

Sterling silver; die formed, fabricated, cast

PHOTO BY ARTIST

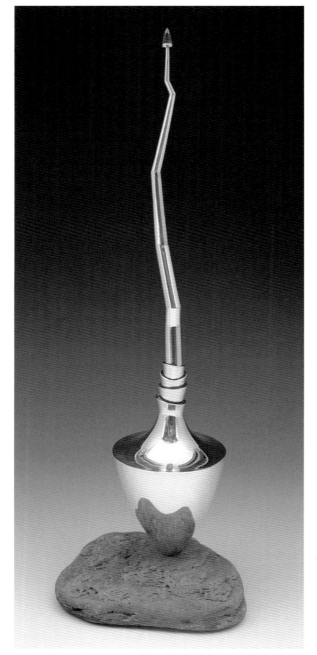

John T. Fix

Spirits Decanter | 2005

14 X 4 X 5 INCHES (35.6 X 10.2 X 12.7 CM)

Sterling silver, 22-karat gold, amethyst, stone; raised, shell formed, fabricated

PHOTO BY ARTIST

Michael and Maureen Banner

Coffee Service, Berkshire Spring | 2004

ENTIRE SET, 18 X 13 X 9 INCHES (45.7 X 33 X 22.9 CM)

Sterling silver, rosewood, enamel; hollow formed, handwrought

PHOTO BY JOHN POLACK

Alberto Zorzi

Fruit Dish | 2000

19¾ X 10 X 11¾ INCHES (50 X 25 X 30 CM)

Sterling silver, iron

PHOTO BY M. SORMONTA
COURTESY OF PAMPALONI GALLERY, FLORENCE, ITALY

Jack da Silva

Silver Basket #1 | 2004

5 X 10 X 10 INCHES (12.7 X 25.4 X 25.4 CM)

Sterling silver; raised, pierced

PHOTO BY M. LEE FATHERREE

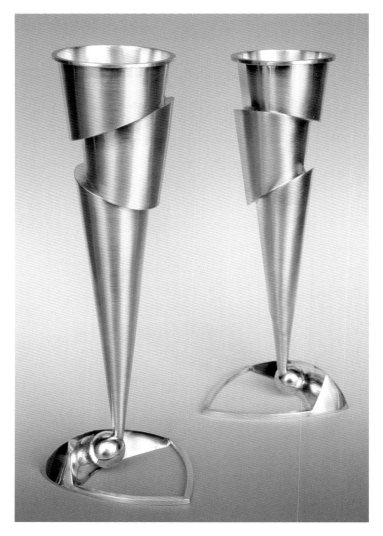

Kenneth C. MacBain

Vases | 2005

EACH, 8 X 3½ X 3 INCHES (20.3 X 8.9 X 7.6 CM)

Sterling silver; constructed

PHOTO BY ARTIST

I designed this bottle to say something about the swirling liquid inside it, and I wanted its shape to echo the Copenhagen skyline. —WY

Wendy Yothers

Spiral Tower Bottle | 1987

11 X 3 INCHES (27.9 X 7.6 CM)
Sterling silver, copper; fused, handwrought
PHOTO BY RICHARD DUANE

David Damkoehler

Celestial Teacups and Wheeled Serving Tray | 2000

13½ X 6¼ X 32½ INCHES (34.3 X 15.9 X 82.6 CM)

Stainless steel; tig welded, cold forged, lathe turned

PHOTOS BY MICHAEL MAU

Alison Counsell

Seedling Tray | 2004

6 X 12 X 12 INCHES (15.2 X 30.5 X 30.5 CM)

Stainless steel; photoetched

PHOTO BY ARTIST

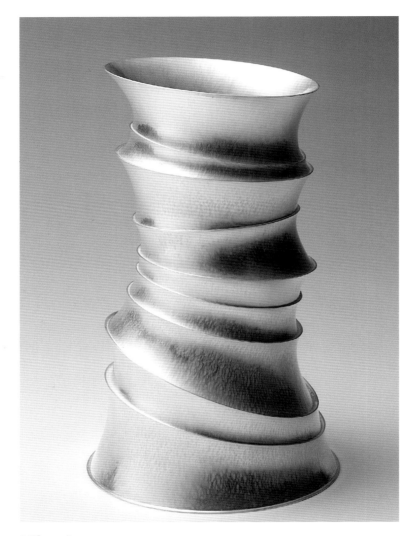

Mihwa Joo

Layer | 2006

8½ X 5 X 5 INCHES (21.6 X 12.7 X 12.7 CM)

Sterling silver; hammered, fabricated

PHOTO BY KWANG-CHOON PARK, KC STUDIO

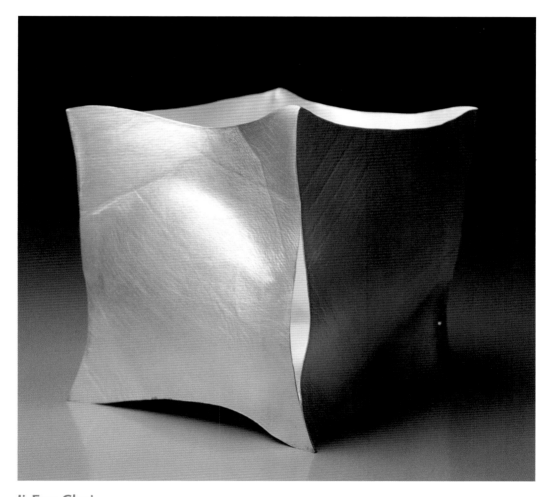

Ji-Eun Choi

Unstable | 2001

7 X 6½ X 7 INCHES (17.8 X 16.5 X 17.8 CM)

Copper, 24-karat gold plating, grapevine; electroformed

PHOTO BY MUNCH STUDIO

Kirk Lang

Venus | 2002

6 X 8½ X 6 INCHES (15.2 X 21.6 X 15.2 CM)

Anodized aluminum, brass, sterling silver, silicone, rubber, pheromones

PHOTOS BY MIKE CIRELLI

Sarah Perkins

Gourd Container | 2005

8 ½ X 6 X 6 INCHES (21.6 X 15.2 X 15.2 CM)

Copper, enamel, sterling silver, fine silver, chalcedony;
raised, fabricated

PHOTO BY ARTIST
COURTESY OF MOBILIA GALLERY, CAMBRIDGE, MASSACHUSETTS

Dale Wedig

Husk | 2002

12 X 24 X 24 INCHES (30.5 X 61 X 61 CM)

Copper, wood, aluminum, silicone; raised, turned, carved, cast

PHOTO BY EDDIE PIESZCHALA

Jan Matthesius

Pomander | 1999

5 X 5 X 5 INCHES (12.7 X 12.7 X 12.7 CM)
Fine silver, aluminum; raised, lathe turned, anodized
PHOTO BY ROB GLASTRA

The pomander holds 12 small containers for collecting scents during your travels. Returning home, you can enjoy your journey once again by checking each scent holder. —JM

Paula J. Newman

Star Anise Havdalah Spice Box | 2003

2 X 10 X 10 INCHES (5.1 X 25.4 X 25.4 CM)

Sterling silver, 22-karat gold, 23-karat gold leaf; hydraulic
die formed, fabricated, hinged, pierced

PHOTO BY M. LEE FATHERREE
COLLECTION OF SCOTT AND NANCY ZACKY

Barbara Bayne

Small Bowls | 2003

LARGEST, 1⅛ X 3¾ X 3½ INCHES (2.9 X 9.5 X 8.9 CM)

Sterling silver; textured, pierced, die formed, fabricated, oxidized

PHOTO BY PAM PERUGI MARRACCINI

Mariah Tuttle

Food for Thought | 2006

6 X 17 X 17 INCHES (15.2 X 43.2 X 43.2 CM)

Copper, patina; sunk, etched, electroformed

PHOTO BY HELEN SHIRK

Ronnie E. DeRutte

Leopard Basin | 2006

6 X 16 X 16 INCHES (15.2 X 40.6 X 40.6 CM)

Bronze, steel, stainless steel, sulfurated potash, potassium dichromate patina, lacquer; lost wax cast, welded, inlaid

PHOTO BY ARTIST
COLLECTION OF MICHAEL FLUSCHE

Bo-Nan Wu

Disorganization | 2006

2 X 6½ X 5½ INCHES (5.1 X 16.5 X 14 CM)

Copper; constructed

PHOTO BY KAREN-LUNG TSAL

My current body of work deals with my longtime interest in ferrous alloys and how they interact when forge welded. Some of the other influences that inform the work, yet are not easy to recognize in the actual pieces, are my interests in geology, geography, architecture, and observation of materials in nature as they are affected by time. When you look into the woods, you see positive and negative space, textural differences, contrasting colors and dimension. My work tries to capture this in a vessel vocabulary. —RS

Rick Smith
Steel Vessel | 1994

18 X 14 X 8 INCHES (45.7 X 35.6 X 20.3 CM)
Wrought iron, mild steel; forged, welded, fabricated

PHOTO BY TOM MILLS

Kathleen A. Brennan
Periphery | 2006
4½ X 6 X 3 INCHES (11.4 X 15.2 X 7.6 CM)
Sterling silver, copper, thermoplastic acrylic resin
PHOTOS BY ARTIST

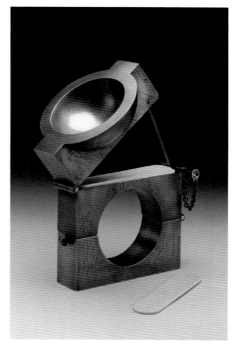

Tara Stephenson

Bulimia Bracelet | 1995

5 X 4 X 3 INCHES (12.7 X 10.2 X 7.6 CM)

Copper, tongue depressors;
fabricated, angle raised, etched

PHOTOS BY SUZANNE COLES

Crys Harse

HRH - Cup of Joy | 2003

5½ X 3¼ X 3¼ INCHES (14 X 8.3 X 8.3 CM)

Sterling silver, jeweler's bronze, brass; formed,
lost wax cast

PHOTO BY ARTIST

Miles Rountree

Not My Year | 2004

8½ X 3½ X 3½ INCHES (21.6 X 8.9 X 8.9 CM)

Copper, bronze; cast, raised

PHOTO BY ROBERT DIAMANTE

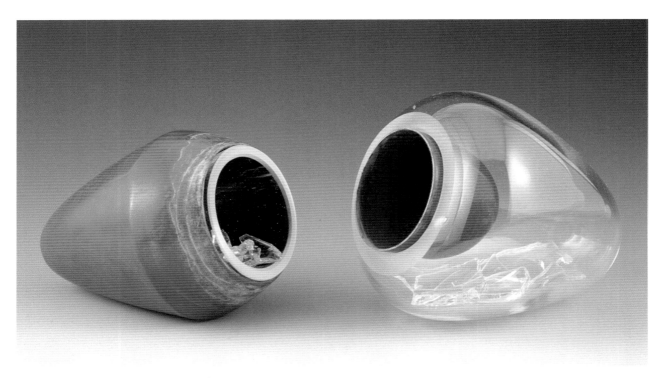

Jennifer Halvorson

Self Portrait | 2004

LEFT, 3¾ X 4 X 3½ INCHES (9.5 X 10.2 X 8.9 CM)
RIGHT, 4 X 4½ X 3½ INCHES (10.2 X 11.4 X 8.9 CM)

Copper, glass; raised, blown

PHOTO BY ARTIST

Lauren B. McAdams
He Said, She Said... | 2005–2006

7 X 29½ X 4 INCHES (17.8 X 75 X 10 CM)

Copper, silver, cubic zirconia; raised, hollow constructed, woven, fabricated

PHOTOS BY ARTIST

Sung-Yeoul Lee

Teapot in Meshed Form | 2006

6 X 8¼ X 7 INCHES (15.2 X 21 X 17.8 CM)

Sterling silver, copper mesh, steel wire

PHOTO BY ARTIST
COLLECTION OF THE SPARTA TEAPOT MUSEUM,
SPARTA, NORTH CAROLINA

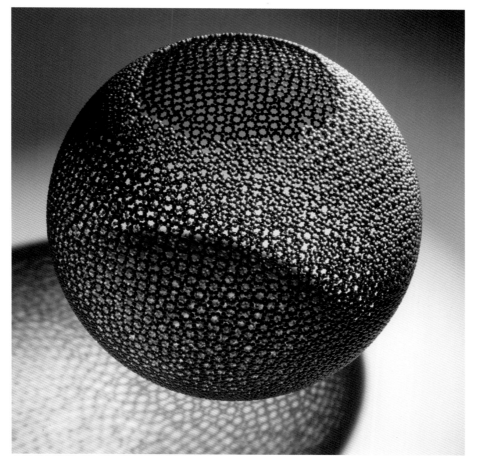

David Huycke

Lace Sphere | 2006

9¾ X 10½ X 10½ INCHES (24.8 X 26.7 X 26.7 CM)

Sterling silver, patina; granulation

PHOTO BY ARTIST

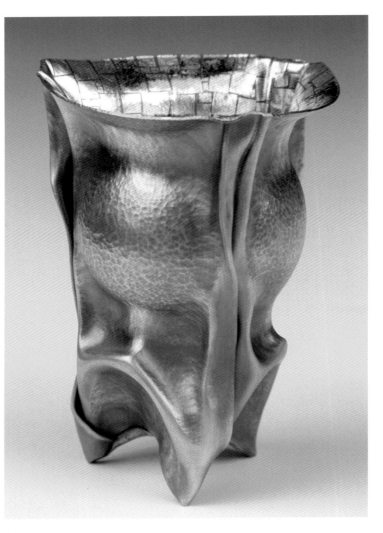

Function is not always at the forefront of my thinking; more the desire to hold, to touch, or gaze. —NGB

Nick Grant Barnes

WA | 2005

5 X 3¼ INCHES (12.7 X 8.3 CM)
Fine silver, 24-karat gold, oxidized patina; fold formed, raised, repoussé, hammered, overlay
PHOTO BY GREG STALEY

Gary Schott

Vessel, 2004

8 X 5 X 5 INCHES (20.3 X 12.7 X 12.7 CM)

Brass, copper, patina; hammer textured, crushed, soldered

PHOTO BY ARTIST

Chris Ramsay

A World View: Insects | 2000

27 X 17 X 17 INCHES (68.6 X 43.2 X 43.2 CM)

Bronze, steel, paint, early 20th century
stereocards of insects, manual focus,
push-button-activated interior light

PHOTOS BY DON WHEELER

Jun Park

Noah's Ark | 2003

7½ X 4 X 5 INCHES (19 X 10.2 X 12.7 CM)

Copper, sterling silver, patina; forged, cast, fabricated, oxidized

PHOTO BY KWANG-CHOON PARK, KC STUDIO

Dong Hyun Kim

Untitled Vessel | 2006

11 X 11¾ X 4½ INCHES (27.9 X 30 X 11.4 CM)

Copper, nickel, wood, black nickel plating; hammered, hand fabricated

PHOTO BY MUNCH STUDIO

Stephen Yusko

Octagonal Oilcan | 2005

8½ X 5½ X 4 INCHES (21.6 X 14 X 10.2 CM)

Steel, tarpaper; forged, fabricated, stacked

PHOTO BY JEFF BRUCE

Saskia Bostelmann

Vessel with Handle | 2002

5 X 2¾ X 3½ INCHES (12.7 X 7 X 8.9 CM)

Sterling silver; formed, forged, hammered, soldered

PHOTO BY ENRIQUE BOSTELMANN

Agnes Chwae

Untitled | 1995

7 X 11 X 11 INCHES (17.8 X 27.9 X 27.9 CM)

Pewter, silver; hammered, fused, soldered

PHOTO BY JIM WILDEMAN
COLLECTION OF ROBERT PFANNEBECKER

Jack da Silva

Silver Bowl | 1998

5 X 12 X 7 INCHES (12.7 X 30.5 X 17.8 CM)

Sterling silver; raised

PHOTO BY ARTIST

This set of bottle-shaped forms can be used as pouring vessels or as vases. The larger, fuller-bodied flask has a pronounced profile seam. In the smaller flask, the front and rear elements meet in a sharply delineated curvilinear seam. I regard the space between and surrounding these flasks as part of the sculptural grouping and consider this space to be as important as that of the individual forms themselves. —DP

Don Porritt

A Pair of Related Flasks/Bottle Forms | 2005–2006

TALLEST, 9¼ X 3 X 3 INCHES (23.5 X 7.6 X 7.6 CM)

Standard silver; raised, seamed construction

PHOTO BY ANDRA NELKI

Peter Verburg

Untitled | 2005

EACH, 3 X 3¾ X 3¾ INCHES (7.6 X 9.5 X 9.5 CM)

Sterling silver; constructed, soldered

PHOTO BY ARTIST

A toolman's special for brewing tea. —*JC*

Jaci Crissman
Nuts and Bolts of Making Tea | 2004

4⅜ X 2½ X 2½ INCHES (11.1 X 6.4 X 6.4 CM)
Silver, nickel silver; fabricated, etched, twined
PHOTOS BY ERICKA CRISSMAN

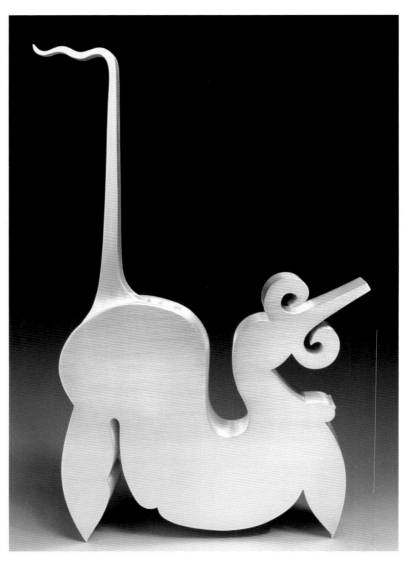

Robly A. Glover

Howling Double-Horned Spring Thing | 2002

11 X 8 X 2½ INCHES (27.9 X 20.3 X 6.4 CM)

Sterling silver; constructed

PHOTO BY ARTIST

David Bausman

Hera | 2005

9 X 10 X 3 INCHES (22.9 X 25.4 X 7.6 CM)

Sterling silver, ebony; die formed, sheet constructed, fabricated, riveted

PHOTO BY ARTIST

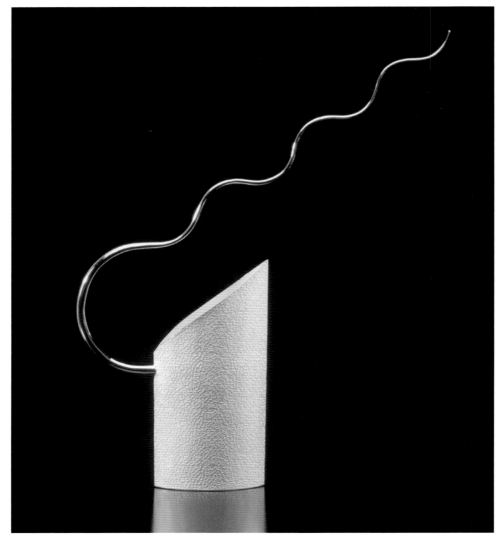

Kevin J. O'Dwyer

Untitled | 1998

18 X 7 X 4 INCHES (45.7 X 17.8 X 10.2 CM)

Sterling silver; formed, forged, fabricated

PHOTO BY JAMES FRAHER

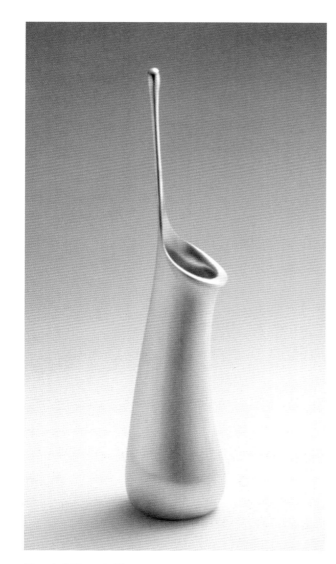

This body of work deals with the physical properties of silver as it appears to transform from solid to liquid state. The forms seem to melt, defying the rules of physics, becoming liquid at room temperature and moving against gravity. The traditional sensibilities of functional silverware give way to a purely sculptural form. I use the inherent qualities of silver, its elasticity, its malleability, and ability to reflect light and shadow to create a sense of liquid motion. —DR

Daniel Randall

Formal Transgression #1 | 2005

11 X 3 X 3 INCHES (27.9 X 7.6 X 7.6 CM)
Fine silver; raised, hollow formed, fabricated
PHOTO BY KWANG-CHOON PARK, KC STUDIO

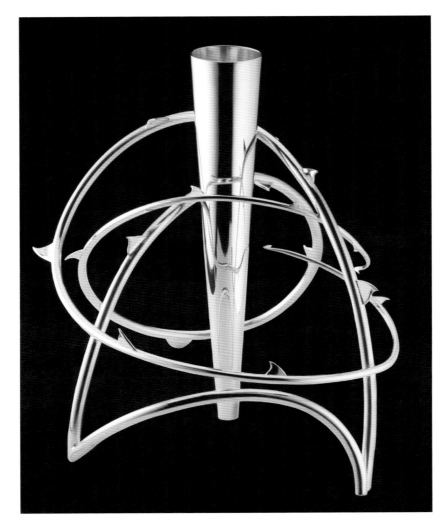

Robyn Nichols

Thorns Bud Vase | 2004

6½ X 6 X 6 INCHES (16.5 X 15.2 X 15.2 CM)

Sterling silver; fabricated, chased, repoussé, raised, forged, polished

PHOTO BY HOLLIS OFFICER

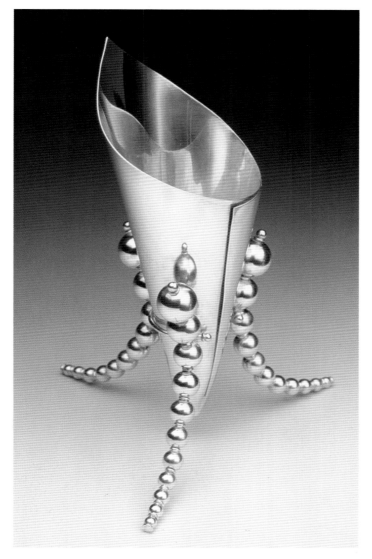

John B. Gilliam

Ibex Vase | 2001

9 X 5 X 5 INCHES (22.9 X 12.7 X 12.7 CM)

Sterling silver; fabricated, soldered

PHOTO BY PETER GROSEBECK

Eduardo Rubio-Arzate

Perfume Bottle | 2004

3¾ X ⅞ X ⅞ INCH (9.5 X 2.2 X 2.2 CM)

Sterling silver, black onyx; fabricated, hollow formed

PHOTO BY MARGOT GEIST

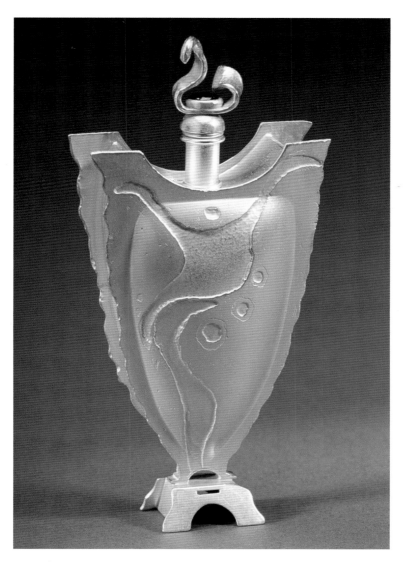

Angela K. Hung

Perfume Bottle | 2003

5 X 1 X 2½ INCHES (12.7 X 2.5 X 6.4 CM)

Sterling silver, fine silver, red stone; forged, hand fabricated, etched, hydraulic pressed

PHOTO BY ARTIST

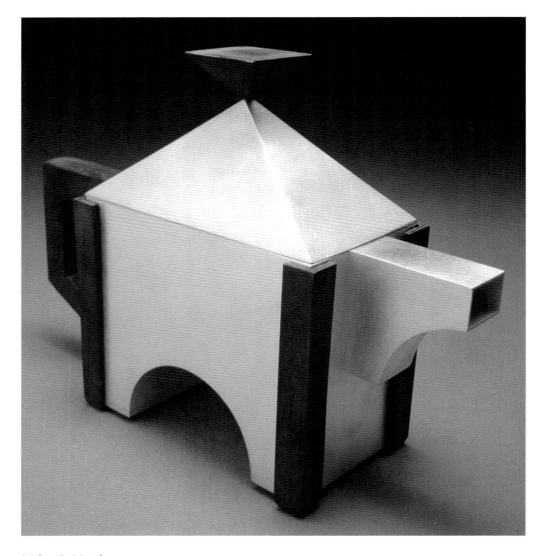

Mike P. Vitale

Architecture Teapot | 2006

7 X 4 X 9 INCHES (17.8 X 10.2 X 22.9 CM)

Sterling silver, Delrin; hollow constructed

PHOTO BY ARTIST

Monika Arendt Fairchild
Untitled | 2006

5 X 6 X 3 INCHES (12.7 X 15.2 X 7.6 CM)
Sterling silver; hand fabricated
PHOTO BY LARRY SANDERS

Stephen Yusko

Mechanics of Solids: Teapot | 2003

4½ X 8 X 3 INCHES (11.4 X 20.3 X 7.6 CM)

Steel; forged, fabricated

PHOTO BY JEFF BRUCE

Sadie Shu-Ping Wang
Copper Rectangle Teapot | 2004

4½ X 2¼ X 3 INCHES (11.4 X 5.7 X 7.6 CM)

Copper, sterling silver; hydraulic die formed,
hand fabricated

PHOTOS BY JOHN LUCAS

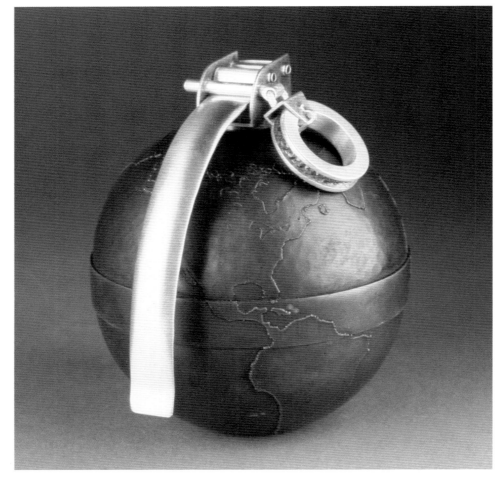

Mitchel T. Martin

B.O.H.I.C.A. | 2003

4 X 4 X 4 INCHES (10.2 X 10.2 X 10.2 CM)

Sterling silver, copper, garnet; raised, electroformed, fabricated

PHOTO BY ARTIST

David A. Huang

Whorled Flow #505 | 2006

2¾ X 3¼ X 3¼ INCHES (7 X 8.3 X 8.3 CM)

Copper, sterling silver, 23-karat gold leaf, patina; raised, chased, gilded

PHOTO BY ARTIST

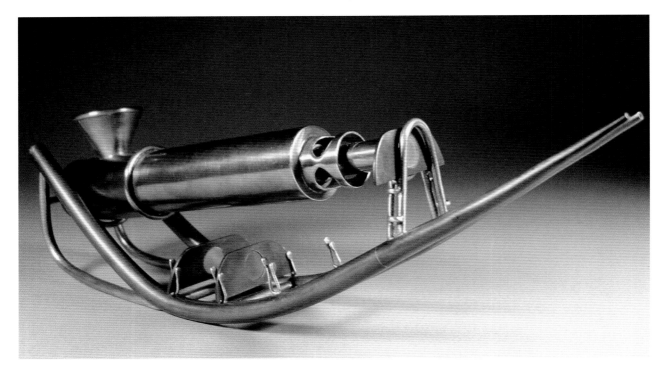

Kathleen A. Brennan

Go On, Take a Closer Look | 2006

5½ X 1 X 3 INCHES (14 X 2.5 X 7.6 CM)

Sterling silver, copper, mirror, colored
thermoplastic acrylic resin

PHOTO BY ARTIST

John E. Cogswell
Bud Vase | 2003

8½ X 3¼ X 3¼ INCHES (21.6 X 8.3 X 8.3 CM)
Sterling silver; fabricated, handwrought
PHOTO BY ARTIST

Lin Stanionis

Untitled | 1996

18 X 5 X 3½ INCHES (45.7 X 12.7 X 8.9 CM)

Bronze, sterling silver, polymer clay; wax cast, constructed

PHOTO BY JIM NEDRESKY

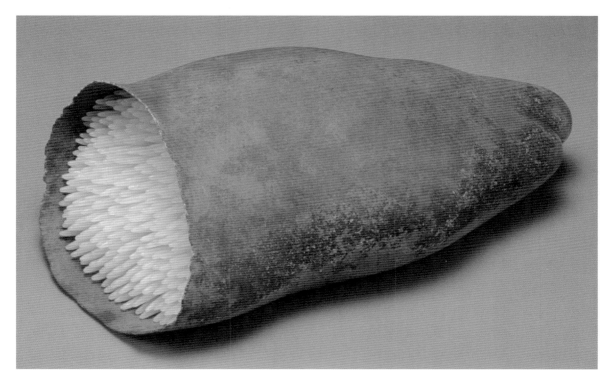

Hsi-Hsia Yang

Bag I | 2002

4 X 6 X 10¾ INCHES (10.2 X 15.2 X 27.3 CM)

Copper, beeswax; raised

PHOTO BY KUN-LUNG, TSAI

Susan R. Ewing
Prague Star Vessel | 2004

7½ X 14 X 11½ INCHES (19 X 35.6 X 29.2 CM)

Copper, brass, patina, gold gilt; raised, fabricated

PHOTO BY JEFFREY SABO

Catherine H. Grisez
Bowl No. Twenty Two | 2001

6½ X 10¾ X 10 INCHES (16.5 X 27.3 X 25.4 CM)
Copper, sterling silver; raised, fabricated
PHOTO BY DOUG YAPLE

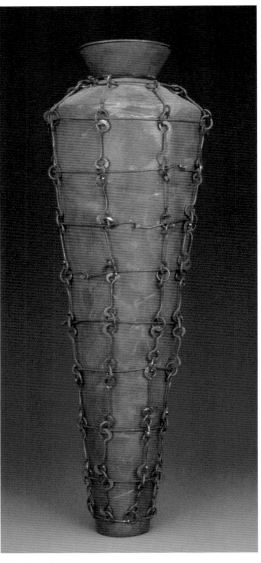

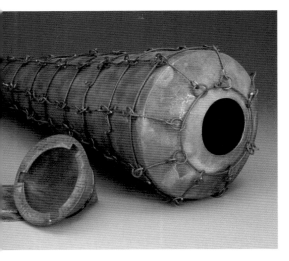

Michael J. Parrett

Bound | 2005

15 X 4 X 4 INCHES (38.1 X 10.2 X 10.2 CM)

Copper, iron, heat patina; raised, fabricated

PHOTOS BY ARTIST

David Griffin

Infrastructure | 2005

14½ X 5 X 5 INCHES (36.8 X 12.7 X 12.7 CM)

Copper, cottonwood, cement; constructed, fabricated, turned, powder coated, cast

PHOTO BY ARTIST

Combining materials, techniques, and concepts allows for the exploration of classical vessel forms by dissecting the various parts of the form: foot, body, shoulder, neck, and mouth. By breaking the form apart and reassigning it a fabricated element, piercing, or other unexpected internal elements, it lures the audience into spending more time in reading the overall composition. —DG

Julie Strauss

Southwest Vessel | 2003

5 X 16 X 16 INCHES (12.7 X 40.6 X 40.6 CM)
Copper; soldered, hammered
PHOTO BY MARSHALL LIND

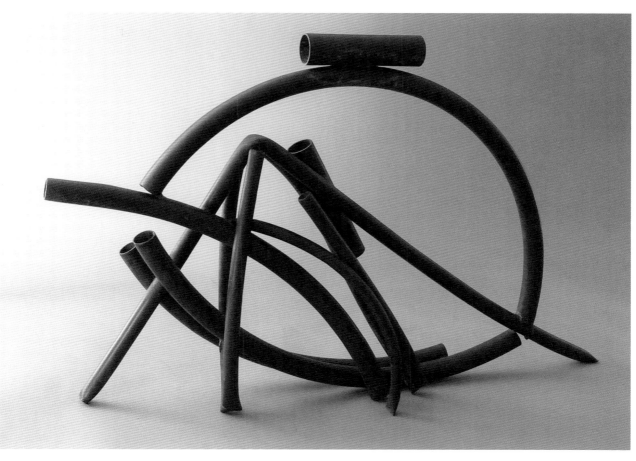

Ishmael H. Soto

Untitled | 2006

20 X 23 X 6 (50.8 X 58.4 X 15.2 CM)

Copper; brazed

PHOTO BY ABIGAIL CHANCE THOMASON

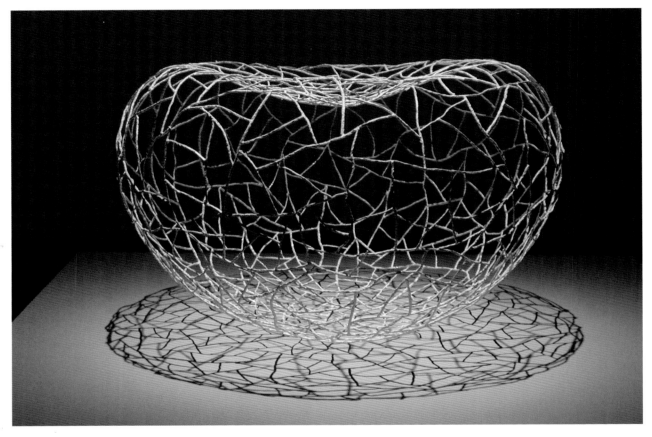

Jenny Edlund

Vessel | 2002

11¾ X 17¾ X 17¾ INCHES (30 X 45.1 X 45.1 CM)

Sterling silver; soldered

PHOTO BY ARTIST

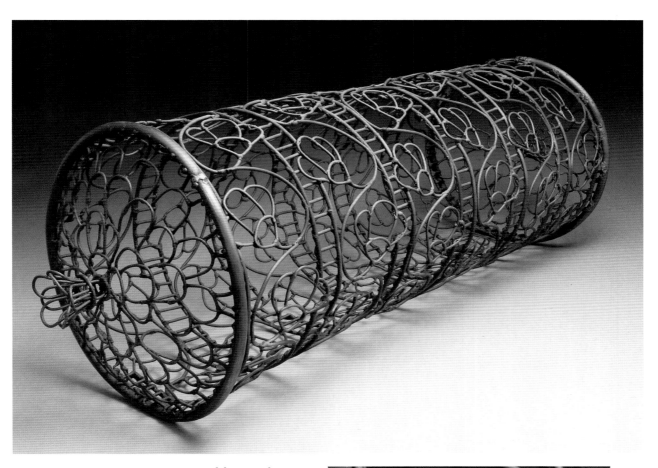

Megan Auman
Pattern Pillow #3 | 2005
9 X 20 X 9 INCHES (22.9 X 50.8 X 22.9 CM)
Copper; welded
PHOTOS BY ARTIST

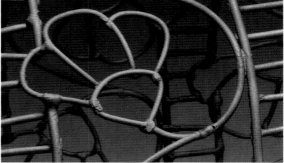

In my work, I demonstrate simple and abstract forms that possess spirit and energy. Nature is the ultimate source for artists. Unconsciously or consciously, people instinctively reach out for things that elicit an emotional response in them. —HK

Hyejeong Ko

Box | 2001

2½ X 4½ X 4½ INCHES (6.4 X 11.4 X 11.4 CM)

Sterling silver; fabricated

PHOTO BY DAN NEUBERGER

Hea Jin Yang

Reminisce About the Good Old Days | 2006

17 X 6 X 6 INCHES (43.2 X 15.2 X 15.2 CM)

Sterling silver; hand fabricated

PHOTO BY MYUNG-WOOK HUH, STUDIO MUNCH

Hanjoo Kim

Pill Container for Respect | 2005

EACH, 9¼ X 2¼ X 2¼ INCHES (23.5 X 5.7 X 5.7 CM)

Sterling silver; fabricated

PHOTO BY MUNCH STUDIO

Wook Koh

Wave | 2003

EACH, 11 X 9¼ X 9¼ INCHES (27.9 X 23.5 X 23.5 CM)

Sterling silver, stainless steel, rubber; raised, scored

PHOTO BY MUNCH STUDIO

Bruce Anderson
Tea Strainer #1 | 2005
2 5/8 X 5 X 4 INCHES (6.7 X 12.7 X 10.2 CM)
Sterling silver; formed, constructed
PHOTO BY RALPH GABRINER

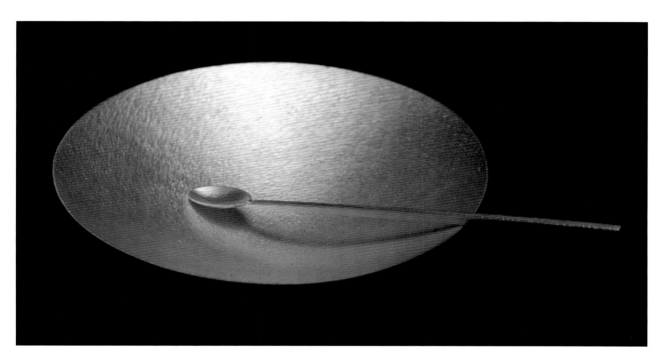

Cathy Chotard

Untitled | 2006

4 X 4 X 4 INCHES (10.2 X 10.2 X 10.2 CM)

Sterling silver; hammered

PHOTO BY ARTIST

Maria Elisabeth Wikström

FF | 2005

10½ X 10 X 5¾ INCHES (26.7 X 25.4 X 14.6 CM)
Sterling silver; fold formed
PHOTO BY TEEMU TÖYRYLÄ

Randy Long

La Madonna Lily Vase | 1998

12 X 4½ X 4½ INCHES (30.5 X 11.4 X 11.4 CM)
Sterling silver; fabricated
PHOTO BY MICHAEL CAVANAGH AND KEVIN MONTAGUE

Ewa Doerenkamp

Untitled | 1999

6¾ X 14¼ X 14¼ INCHES (17 X 36 X 36 CM)

Gilding metal; raised, silver plated

PHOTO BY ARTIST

Daniel Randall

Formal Transgression #3 | 2005

3 X 4 X 2 INCHES (7.6 X 10.2 X 5.1 CM)

Fine silver; raised, hollow formed, fabricated

PHOTO BY KWANG-CHOON PARK, KC STUDIO

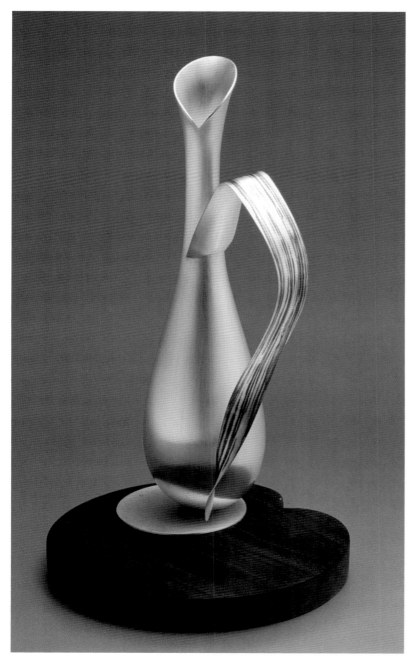

Heather Bayless

Bulb Cruet | 2005

6 ¾ X 4 ¾ X 4 ¾ INCHES (17.1 X 12 X 12 CM)

Sterling silver, fine silver, copper, wood; mokume gane, hammered, hand fabricated

PHOTO BY KWANG-CHOON PARK, KC STUDIO

Leslie Matthews

Scapula Vessels | 2005

EACH, 3³/₁₆ X 3³/₁₆ X 2¾ INCHES (8 X 8 X 7 CM)

Sterling silver

PHOTO BY GRANT HANCOCK

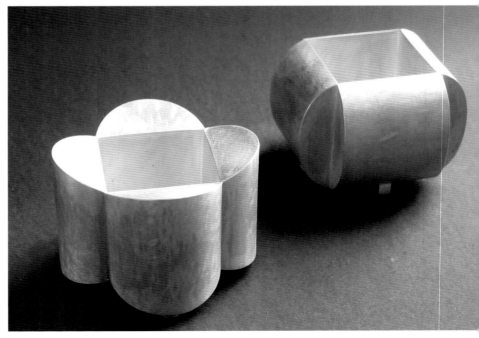

Peter Verburg

Untitled | 2005

EACH, 3 X 4¼ X 4¼ INCHES (7.6 X 10.8 X 10.8 CM)

Sterling silver; constructed, soldered

PHOTO BY ARTIST

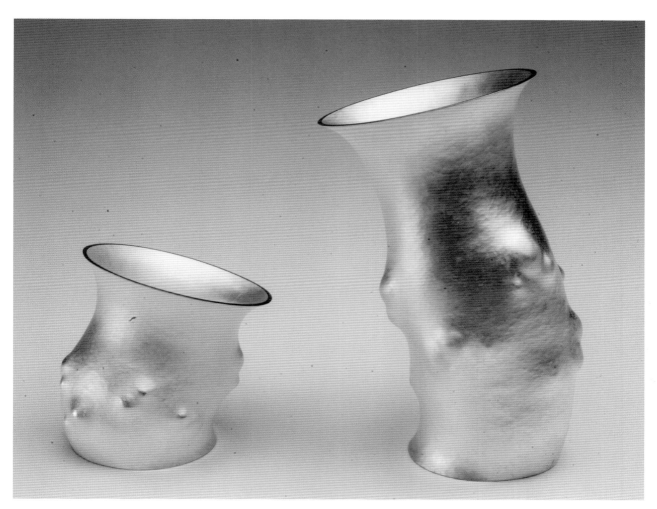

Li-Sheng Cheng

Mutation | 2006

3½ X 2 X 2 INCHES (8.9 X 5.1 X 5.1 CM)

Sterling silver; repoussé, raised, fabricated

PHOTO BY ARTIST

Julie Blyfield
Pod Vessels | 2004

TALLEST, 5⅛ X 2½ X 2½ INCHES (13 X 6.5 X 6.5 CM)
Pure silver, copper; oxidized, wax finish

PHOTO BY GRANT HANCOCK
COURTESY OF GALLERY FUNAKI, MELBOURNE, AUSTRALIA

Brigid O'Hanrahan

Untitled | 2001

EACH, 2⅝ X 2¼ X 2¼ INCHES (6.7 X 5.7 X 5.7 CM)

Fine silver, 22-karat gold; angle raised, inlaid

PHOTO BY ARTIST

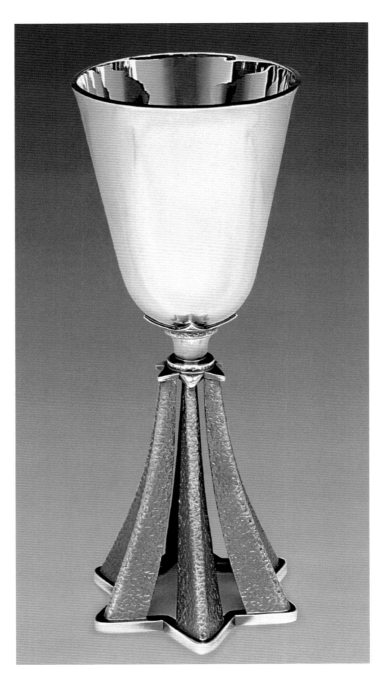

John E. Cogswell

Kiddush Cup | 2006

6¾ X 3 INCHES (17.1 X 7.6 CM)

Sterling silver; raised, fabricated, handwrought

PHOTO BY ARTIST

Eduardo Rubio-Arzate

Perfume Bottle | 2004

3 ½ X ⅞ X ⅞ INCH (8.9 X 2.2 X 2.2 CM)

Sterling silver, jasper, black onyx; fabricated, hollow formed

PHOTO BY MARGOT GEIST

Agnes Pal

Wallenburg Safehouse | 2002

3 X 2½ X 2½ INCHES (7.6 X 6.4 X 6.4 CM)

Sterling silver, iron; cast, constructed, chased, damascened

PHOTO BY ARTIST

Kate Cathey

Thistle Honey Pot & Dipper | 2002

3½ X 3¼ X 3¼ INCHES (8.9 X 8.3 X 8.3 CM)

Sterling silver, fine silver, enamel, walnut; etched,
roll printed, formed, soldered, riveted

PHOTO BY ROBERT DIAMANTE

Fred Fenster

Teapot | 1990

11 X 8½ X 6 INCHES (27.9 X 21.6 X 15.2 CM)

Pewter; raised, constructed

PHOTO BY ARTIST

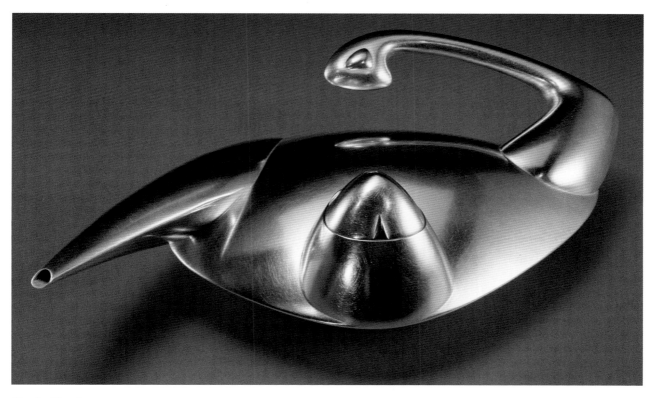

Cody Bush

Derelict | 1998

6 X 11 X 5½ INCHES (15.2 X 27.9 X 14 CM)

Sterling silver; hydraulic die formed

PHOTO BY ARTIST

Kimberlie J. Moy
Untitled (Tea Set) | 2005

TEAPOT, 7 X 14 X 5 INCHES (17.8 X 35.6 X 12.7 CM)
EACH CUP, 3 X 2 X 1½ INCHES (7.6 X 5.1 X 3.8 CM)

Sterling silver; formed, fabricated, reticulated

PHOTO BY ARTIST

James Obermeier

Sanctuary Pouring Vessel and Cups | 2001

VESSEL, 10½ X 4¾ X 3 INCHES (26.7 X 12 X 7.6 CM)

Sterling silver, copper, steel, 14-karat gold, patina; raised, stretched, forged

PHOTO BY KEVIN MONTAGUE

These two versions show contrasting details in the surface appearance of the flutes. One has a hammer texture, the other has a surface created by the casting process. In both designs, the handgrips provide efficient and comfortable handling characteristics. —DP

Don Porritt

Fluted Flagons | 2002

TALLEST, 8⅝ X 2⅝ X 2⅝ INCHES (21.9 X 6.7 X 6.7 CM)

Standard silver, gold plate; seamed, fabricated

PHOTO BY ANDRA NELKI

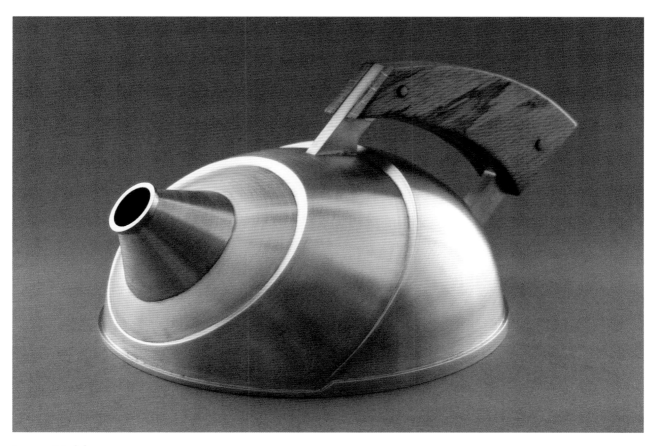

Jason Noble

Pewter Teapot | 2005

4½ X 7 X 10 INCHES (11.4 X 17.8 X 25.4 CM)

Pewter, oak, steel; spun, formed, fused, soldered

PHOTO BY ARTIST

Curtis K. LaFollette

Rust Belt Tea Strainer | 2006

5 X 4¼ X 6½ INCHES (12.7 X 10.8 X 16.5 CM)

Sterling silver, rosewood, brass, stainless
steel, mild steel; raised, fabricated

PHOTO BY BOB NASH

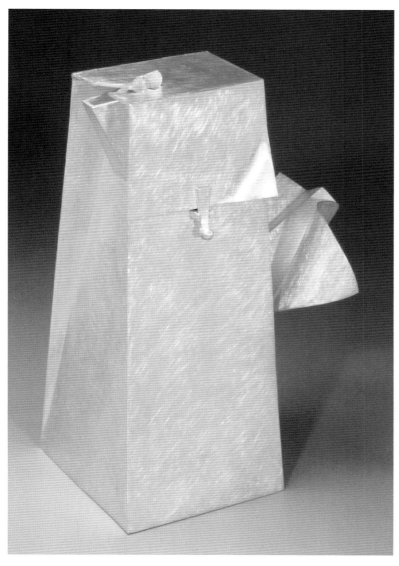

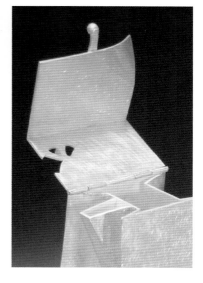

Yoko Noguchi
Origami Teapot | 2006
5 X 3½ X 2 INCHES (12.7 X 8.9 X 5.1 CM)
Sterling silver; fabricated
PHOTOS BY ARTIST

Michelle Ritter

Passion | 2003

9 X 8 X 6 INCHES (22.9 X 20.3 X 15.2 CM)

Silver; raised, formed, die formed,
fabricated, soldered, oxidized

PHOTO BY HELEN SHIRK

Wendy Yothers

Tea at Hattie's | 2006

14 X 12 INCHES (35.6 X 30.5 CM)

830 silver; hand raised, fabricated

PHOTO BY RICHARD DUANE

Although the windows are recessed, they are sealed. The pot is functional. The weathervane twirls with a slight puff of wind. —WY

Munya Avigail Upin

934 7th Avenue | 1983

3 X 6½ X 5 INCHES (7.6 X 16.5 X 12.7 CM)

Sterling silver, nickel; raised, fabricated, married metal

PHOTO BY ARTIST

David Damkoehler
Breadbasket for Joseph Holtzman | 2004

11 X 24 X 24 INCHES (27.9 X 61 X 61 CM)
Stainless steel; tig welded, drilled
PHOTO BY DEAN POWELL

Breadbasket for Joseph Holtzman *has a strong presence on any table. Created from 42 Volrath serving forks, the tines have been covered with stainless balls and welded into the base. I dedicated the bowl to Joseph A. Holtzman, founder of* Nest *magazine and a Christopher Dresser fanatic who challenges all notions of good design.* —DD

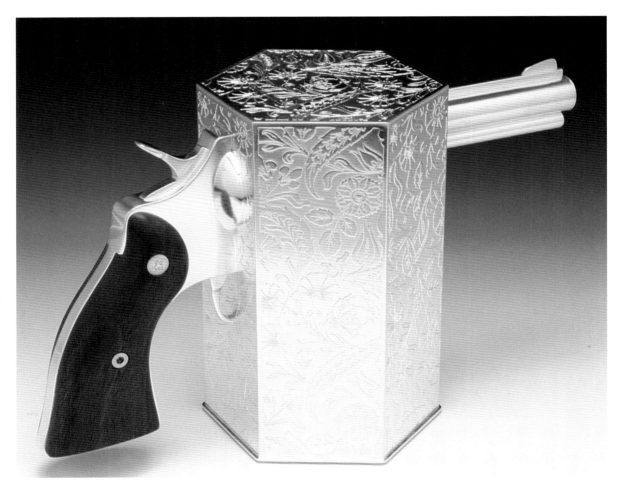

Jeffrey Clancy

Tea for One | 2002

6 X 4 X 10 INCHES (15.2 X 10.2 X 25.4 CM)
Sterling silver, mahogany; fabricated

PHOTOS BY ARTIST

Hratch Babikian
No Guns at the Dinner Table | 2000

4 X 4 X 4 INCHES (10.2 X 10.2 X 10.2 CM)
Bronze, toy gun parts; hollow formed, fabricated
PHOTOS BY S. GROSSBECK

Noël Yovovich

Just My Cup of Tea | 2004

6 X 5 X 3 INCHES (15.2 X 12.7 X 7.6 CM)

Sterling silver, copper, titanium, 14-karat gold, tourmalines, diamonds, carnelian, porcelain, stoneware, glass; etched, constructed

PHOTOS BY LARRY SANDERS

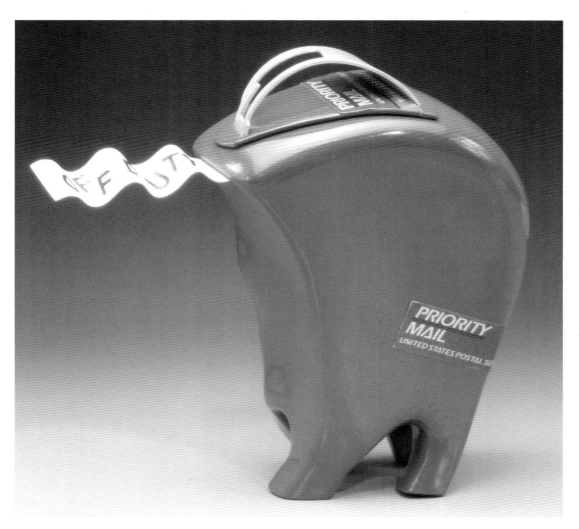

Yoko Noguchi

9–5 Mailbox Pitcher | 2006

5 X 5 X 2½ INCHES (12.7 X 12.7 X 6.4 CM)

Copper, sterling silver; electroformed, powder coated

PHOTO BY ARTIST

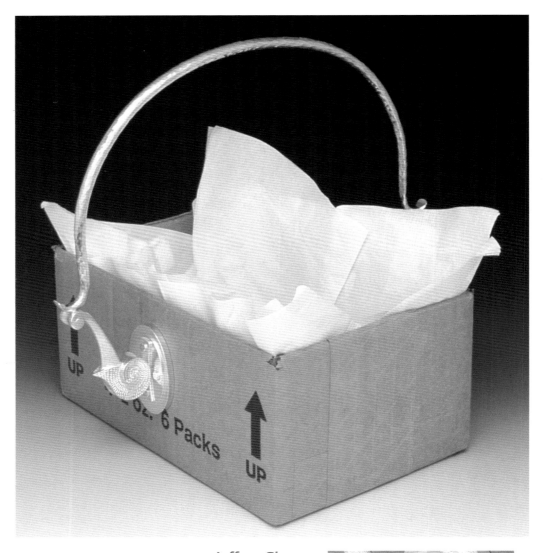

Jeffrey Clancy

Bread for All | 2003

12 X 11 X 9½ INCHES (30.5 X 27.9 X 24.1 CM)

Sterling silver, cardboard, napkin; forged, cast, fabricated

PHOTOS BY ARTIST

Claas Eicke Kuhnen

CoffeeTime - Social Time (finale) | 2006

MUG, 6 X 9 X 4½ INCHES (15.2 X 22.9 X 11.4 CM)
CREAMER, 3½ X 3½ X 1½ INCHES (8.9 X 8.9 X 3.8 CM)

Paper cup, wenge wood, sterling silver, nickel silver; fabricated,
raised, hydraulic die formed, stamped, hammered, textured

PHOTO BY KEITH MEISER

Katie Poliquin

Banana Box | 2005

4 X 8¼ X 1½ INCHES (10.2 X 21 X 3.8 CM)

Copper, brass, magnet, sticker, pigment; hollow constructed

PHOTOS BY ROBERT DIAMANTE

Roberta A. Williamson and David E. Williamson

Breakfast Cheer | 2004

14 X 6 X 6 INCHES (35.6 X 15.2 X 15.2 CM)

Found object coffee tin, tin ballerina, sterling silver, wood,
vintage tin cup; fabricated, assembled

PHOTO BY JERRY ANTHONY

Loretta Fontaine

Pop Can Trio | 2006

TALLEST, 5 X 1¾ X 1½ INCHES (12.6 X 4.4 X 3.8 CM)

Recycled aluminum cans, waxed cotton; sewn

PHOTO BY ARTIST

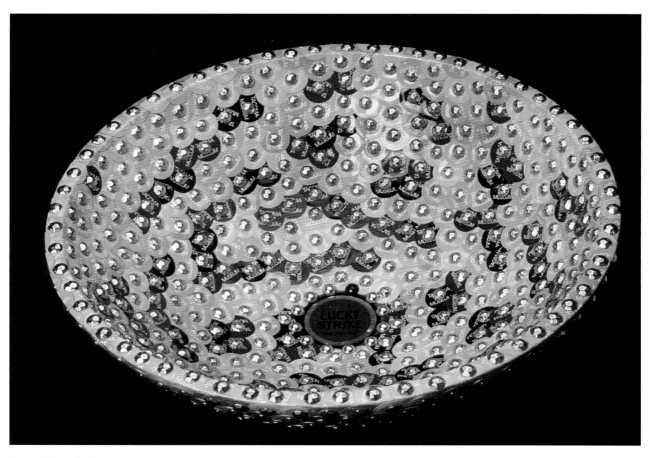

Jean Mandeberg

Lucky Strike | 2006

6 X 17 X 16 INCHES (15.2 X 43.2 X 40.6 CM)

Tin museum tags, steel tacks, wood

PHOTO BY MICHAEL RYAN

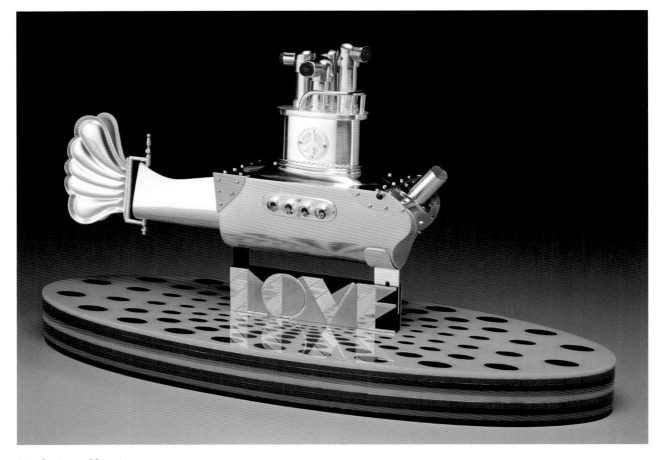

Linda Lee Shapiro

Peace and Love in the Yellow Sub | 2005

11¼ X 18 X 7 INCHES (28.6 X 45.7 X 17.8 CM)

Sterling silver, brass, gold, acrylic; formed, fabricated

PHOTO BY ARTIST

Boris Bally

Man in Stereo: The Muybridge Platters | 2001

EACH, 25 X 60 X 4 INCHES (63.5 X 152.4 X 10.2 CM)
Recycled traffic signs, copper, steel bolt; hand spun,
lathe turned, riveted, pierced
PHOTO BY DEAN POWELL

Becky I. Chader

Lakefront Defense: A Reliquary for Mosquito Repellant | 2000

15 X 11 X 11 INCHES (38.1 X 27.9 X 27.9 CM)

Copper, sterling silver, glass, citronella, repellent; cast, fabricated

PHOTO BY ALAN MCCOY

Harlan W. Butt

Earth Beneath Our Feet: Spider Jar | 2005

6½ X 4 X 4 INCHES (16.5 X 10.2 X 10.2 CM)

Silver, enamel, copper; raised, cloisonné, etched, fabricated

PHOTO BY RAFAEL MOLINA

The shaker is attached to the extension arm; itching powder is loaded into the shaker. The arm is then extended and shaken over the victim. —ND

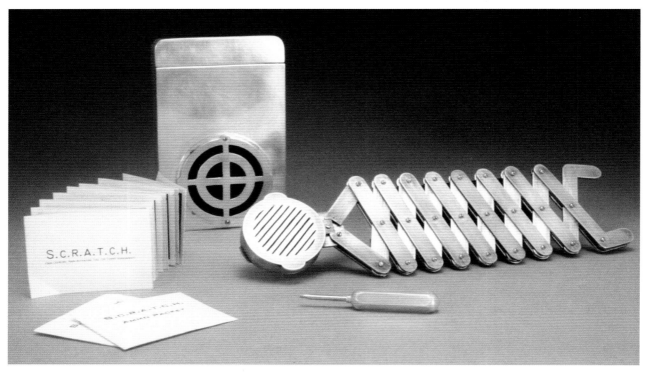

Nathan Dube

S.C.R.A.T.C.H. (Skin Crawling, Rash Activating Tool for Covert Harassment) | 2006

5 X 3 X 1 INCH (12.7 X 7.6 X 2.5 CM)

Silver, itching powder; fabricated, flocked

PHOTOS BY ARTIST

Tara Stephenson

Chocolate Relationship | 1995

3 ½ X 4 X 3 INCHES (8.9 X 10.2 X 7.6 CM)

Copper, sterling silver, thermoplastic mirror, chocolate; fabricated, hydraulic die formed

PHOTOS BY SUZANNE COLES

Tzadaka boxes are traditional judaica pieces that symbolize charity and giving. This box is made in the spirit of a birdhouse. I think of birdhouses my grandfather built and a correlation with the giving spirit. —TRM

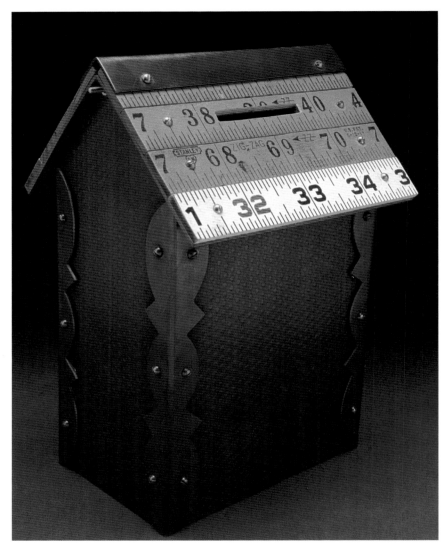

Tedd R. McDonah
Tzadaka Box | 2004

8 X 5 X 3 INCHES (20.3 X 12.7 X 7.6 CM)
Copper, wooden ruler parts; roll printed, scored, folded, cold connected, screwed

PHOTO BY BECKY MCDONAH

Chris Ramsay

Extinct | 2001

15 X 12 X 11 INCHES (38.1 X 30.5 X 27.9 CM)

Copper, steel, globe, postage stamps, resin, found objects

PHOTOS BY DON WHEELER

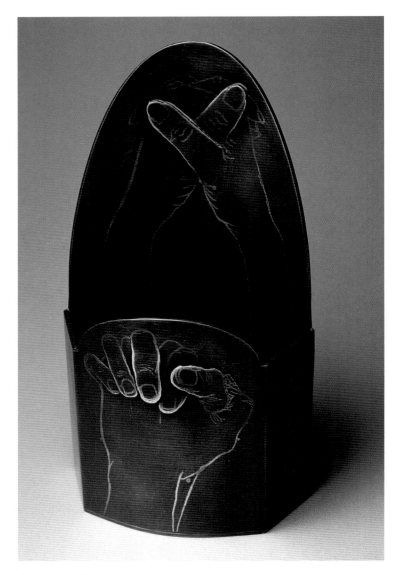

Soo Mee Lim

Hope and Pray | 2005

4 ¼ X 2 ¾ X 7 ¾ INCHES (10.8 X 7 X 19.7 CM)

Copper

PHOTO BY MYUNG-WOOK HUH, STUDIO MUNCH

As a metalsmith, I am drawn to industrial debris as someone else might be drawn to pirate's treasure. I find great satisfaction in taking these work-worn metal parts and transforming them into vessels that could become a valued part of our living space. Visible hammer marks and rivets in the finished piece often reflect the industrial origin of its components. —CH

Crys Harse

Ravensdean School of Music | 2006

5½ X 3¼ X 3¼ INCHES (14 X 8.3 X 8.3 CM)

Recycled copper, brass; pierced, constructed, riveted, photoetched

PHOTO BY NELSON VIGNEAULT

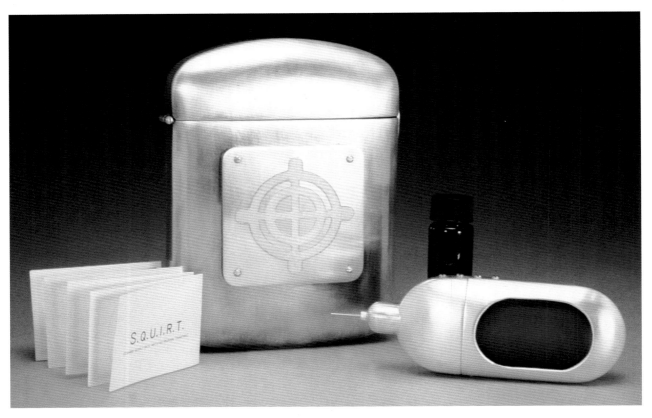

Nathan Dube

S.Q.U.I.R.T. (Staining Quickly Until Irritating Response Transpires) | 2006

5 X 3½ X 1⅜ INCHES (12.7 X 8.9 X 3.5 CM)

Silver, disappearing ink, glass tubes, plastic bottles; die formed, fabricated, flocked

PHOTO BY ARTIST

The squirter is loaded by inserting the tip into the ammo bottle and the ink is sucked up. The squirter is then fired at the victim. —ND

Renée Zettle-Sterling
Study in the Ephemera #12 | 2006

5½ X 6½ X 10¼ INCHES (14 X 16.5 X 26 CM)
Silver, bronze, brass, rubber, bubble solution, air;
fabricated, cast

PHOTOS BY DAVID SMITH

Boris Bally
Bin There! | 2004

EACH, 18 X 11½ X 8 INCHES (45.7 X 29.2 X 20.3 CM)

Recycled aluminum traffic signs, copper; hand roll formed, brake formed, cold joined, riveted, trapped tongue in groove

PHOTOS BY ARTIST

Thomas Smith

Positive/Negative | 2006

4 X 2 X 2 INCHES (10.2 X 5.1 X 5.1 CM)

Gilding metal, enamel spray paint, Lazertran image;
scored, folded, soldered

PHOTO BY ARTIST

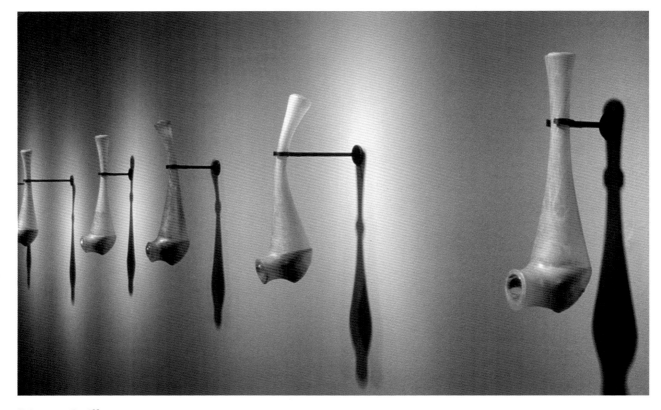

Dianne Reilly

Chronology of Awareness | 2003

EACH, 6 X 9 X 8 INCHES (15.2 X 22.9 X 20.3 CM)

Fine silver, brass, enamel, resin, acrylic, intestine, pigment;
raised, electroformed, lathe worked, constructed

PHOTO BY ARTIST

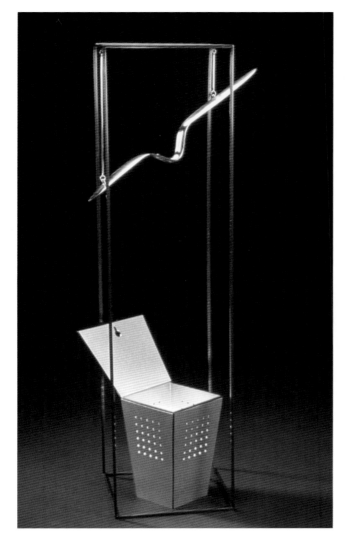

Wings have long been used as a symbol of freedom. Through an image of a wing, I wish to express an inner experience of mind, a free will that seeks escape from the confinement of reality. In building the wing, fusing in my inner experience was of more importance than investigating the detailed form. Light was used to stress the image being extended into space and to express free will. —EKA

Eun-Kyung An
A Wish | 2001

20 X 10 X 7 INCHES (50.8 X 25.4 X 17.8 CM)
Copper, brass, aluminum, sterling silver; anodized
PHOTO BY MYUNG-WOOK HUH, MUNCH STUDIO

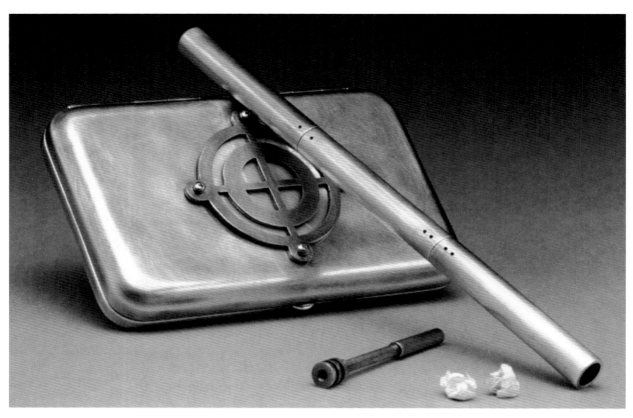

Nathan Dube

S.P.I.T. (Saliva and Paper Instigating Trauma) | 2005

4¾ X 7 X 2¾ INCHES (12 X 17.8 X 7 CM)

Silver, paper, mother-of-pearl; die formed, fabricated

PHOTOS BY ARTIST

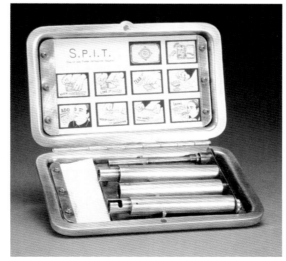

The shooter is assembled; a piece of paper is pulled and crumpled into a ball, then fired using the tube. —ND

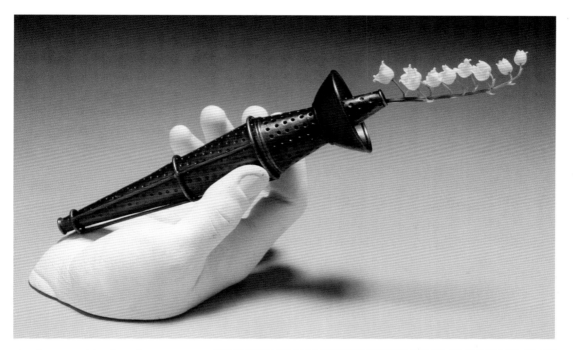

Andrew L. Kuebeck

Spitter Straw, 2006

7½ X 1½ X 1½ INCHES (19 X 3.8 X 3.8 CM)

Copper, liver-of-sulfur patina; fabricated, reticulated

PHOTOS BY TOM P. MUIR

Yeonkyung Kim

Step by Step | 2001

3 X 3 X 2 INCHES (7.6 X 7.6 X 5.1 CM)

Silver

PHOTOS BY MYUNG-WOOK HUH

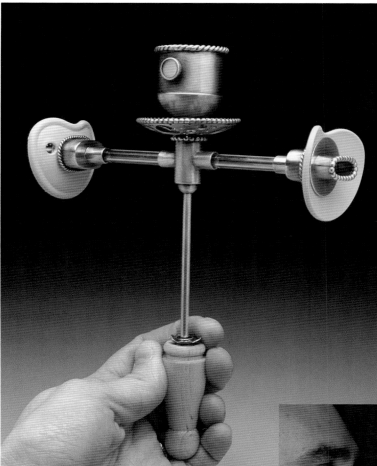

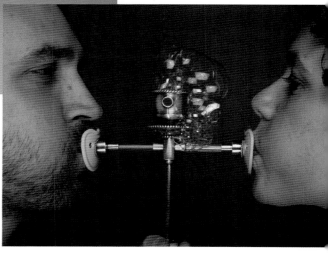

Renée Zettle-Sterling

Study in the Ephemeral #6 | 2006

6½ X 7 X 2 INCHES (16.5 X 17.8 X 5.1 CM)

Silver, found objects, wood, bubble solution,
air; fabricated

PHOTOS BY DAVID SMITH

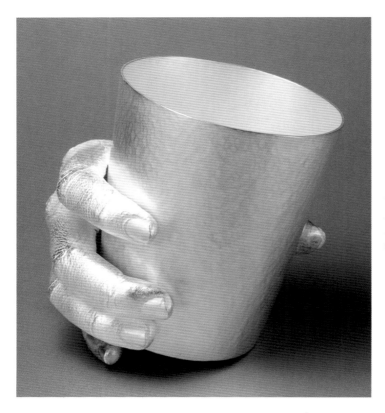

◀ **Soo Mee Lim**

Hand in Hand | 2004

3¼ X 4½ X 4½ INCHES (8.3 X 11.4 X 11.4 CM)
Silver
PHOTO BY MYUNG-WOOK HUH, STUDIO MUNCH

▼ **Tamar Kern**

Offering of Artist's Hands | 2002

5 X 3 X 3 INCHES (12.7 X 7.6 X 7.6 CM)
Silver plated copper
PHOTO BY ARTIST

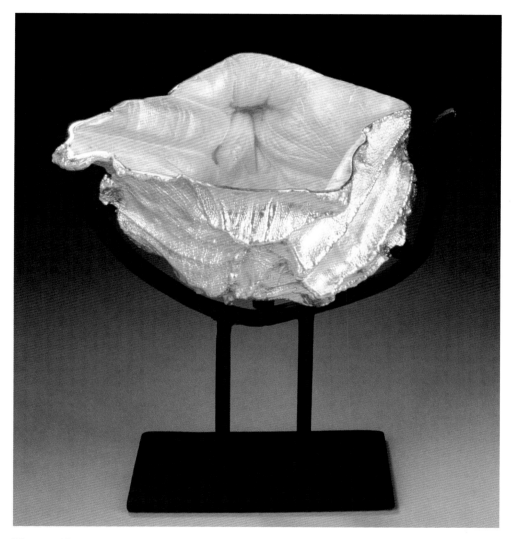

Tamar Kern

Michelle & Eliot | 2004

11 X 7½ X 4½ INCHES (27.9 X 19 X 11.4 CM)

Silver, steel

PHOTO BY ARTIST

Eric McKinley

Unused Change | 2005

5 X 6½ X 4½ INCHES (12.7 X 16.5 X 11.4 CM)

Pennies, copper; soldered, cut

PHOTO BY ARTIST

Ishmael H. Soto

Untitled | 2006

30 X 26 X 17½ INCHES (76.2 X 66 X 44.5 CM)

Copper; brazed

PHOTO BY ABIGAIL CHANCE THOMASON

Sun Kyoung Kim

Hope for a Fruition | 2003

22 X 11 X 6 INCHES (55.9 X 27.9 X 15.2 CM)

Copper, silver; fabricated

PHOTO BY ARTIST

Thomas Mann

Menagerie Teapot | 2000

15½ X 18 X 5 INCHES (39.4 X 45.7 X 12.7 CM)

Bronze, brass, steel, patina

PHOTO BY GERARD PERRONE

Eun Yeong Jeong

Illusion | 2006

10 X 12½ X 9½ INCHES (25.4 X 31.8 X 22.9 CM)

Sterling silver, magnifying glass, mirror, photograph; fabricated

PHOTO BY ARTIST

Dennis Nahabetian
Vessel #83 | 2006

7 X 7 X 7 INCHES (17.8 X 17.8 X 17.8 CM)
Copper, bronze, patina, polychrome
PHOTOS BY ARTIST

I love using traditional materials in unexpected ways. This coarsely textured steel wool vessel showcases the contrasting softness of the material. —KJL

Karen J. Lauseng
Untitled | *2006*

10 X 8½ X 8½ INCHES (25.4 X 21.6 X 21.6 CM)
Steel wool, sterling silver
PHOTO BY ARTIST

David Huycke

Pearl Chaos | 2006

6 X 6½ X 6½ INCHES (15.2 X 16.5 X 16.5 CM)
Sterling silver, patina; granulation
PHOTO BY ARTIST

From its ancient origins, granulation has been used primary as decoration. These pieces utilize granulation as a constructive, structural technique. The grains simultaneously form the object and its artistic impression. These works also have a philosophical dimension that raises such issues as chaos and order, and the formal similarity of the part and the whole. —DH

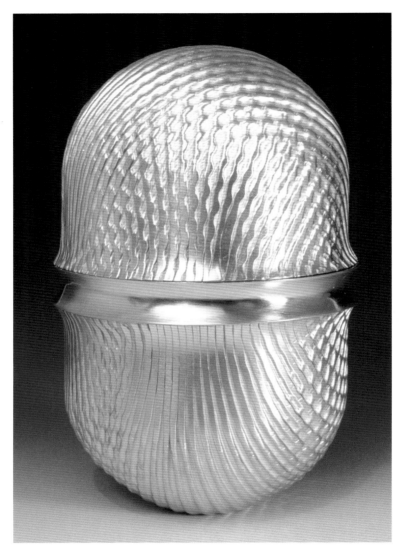

Cynthia Eid

Convergences II | 2002

4 X 2 X 2 INCHES (10.2 X 5.1 X 5.1 CM)

Argentium sterling silver; microfolded, deep drawn in
hydraulic press, hammer formed, constructed

PHOTO BY ARTIST

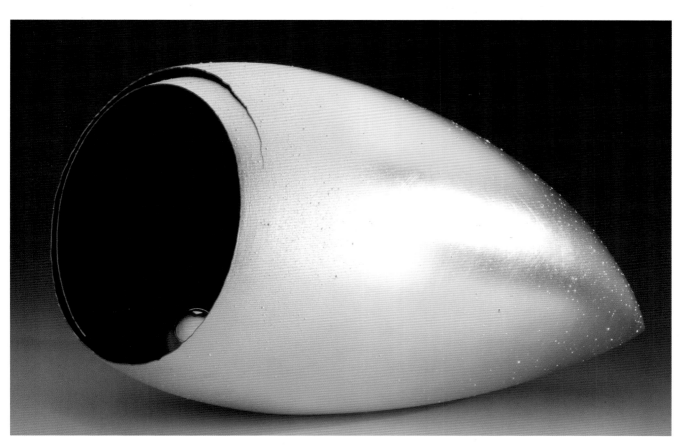

Jan Matthesius

Treasure of New Life | 2006

12 X 12 X 23 INCHES (30.5 X 30.5 X 58.4 CM)

Fine silver, sterling silver; electroformed

PHOTO BY ROB GLASTRA

Tan-Chi Dandy Chao

Dead end • as always • in blossom | 2002

10 X 10 X 12½ INCHES (25.4 X 25.4 X 31.8 CM)

Sterling silver, copper, patina; raised

PHOTO BY ARTIST

Brigid O'Hanrahan

Untitled | 1998

4½ X 5 X 5 INCHES (11.4 X 12.7 X 12.7 CM)

Silver, copper; angle raised, constructed, soldered

PHOTO BY ARTIST

Gail Ralston
Running Cups | 2002

EACH, 3¼ X 2 X 2 INCHES (8.3 X 5.1 X 5.1 CM)
Fine silver, sterling silver; raised, fabricated

PHOTOS BY SARAH PERKINS

Daniel Randall

Formal Transgression #2 | 2005

4 X 5 X 2½ INCHES (10.2 X 12.7 X 6.4 CM)

Fine silver; raised, hollow formed, fabricated

PHOTO BY KWANG-CHOON PARK, KC STUDIO

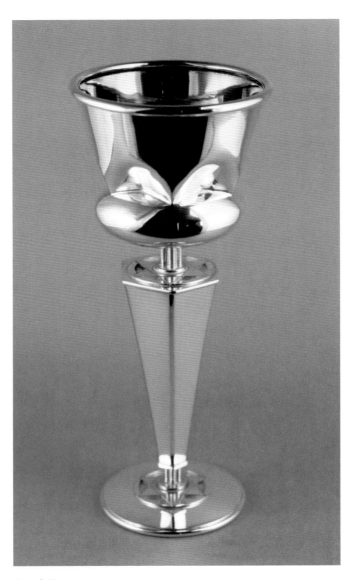

Fred Fenster

Star Kiddush Cup | 1998

8 X 3 X 3 INCHES (20.3 X 7.6 X 7.6 CM)

Sterling silver; raised, constructed

PHOTO BY ARTIST

Jiwon Han

Untitled | 1998

6¾ X 3⅛ X 3⅛ INCHES (17.1 X 7.6 X 7.6 CM)

Sterling silver, 18-karat gold; raised, formed

PHOTO BY KAREN BELL

Kerstin Becker

Bowls | 2003

LARGER, 5 X 5 X 2¾ INCHES (12.7 X 12.7 X 7 CM)

Silver

PHOTO BY EVA JÜNGER

Hratch Babikian
Martini for 2 | 2006

5 X 3 X 3 INCHES (12.7 X 7.6 X 7.6 CM)
Silver; cast, hollow formed, fabricated, forged
PHOTO BY ARTIST

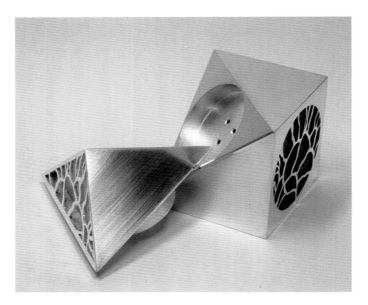

Meghan R. Wagg
Salt and Pepper Shakers | 2006

1⅝ X 1¾ X 1¾ INCHES (4.1 X 4.3 X 4.3 CM)
Sterling silver; formed, soldered, lathe turned
PHOTO BY ARTIST

The shakers fit together to form a cube. —MRW

Hanjoo Kim
3+4, 5, 6 | 2002

EACH, 2½ X 1½ X 1½ INCHES (6.4 X 3.8 X 3.8 CM)
Sterling silver; fabricated
PHOTO BY MUNCH STUDIO

Oliver Smith

Fondue | 2002

8 X 8 X 9 INCHES (20.3 X 20.3 X 22.9 CM)

950 silver, sterling silver, Monel, stainless
steel, Teflon, silicon fiber; hammered

PHOTO BY SEAN BOOTH

Kenneth C. MacBain

Tea and Coffee Set | 2005

COFFEE POT, 10 X 11½ X 4½ INCHES (25.4 X 29.2 X 11.4 CM)
TEAPOT, 9½ X 10½ X 4 INCHES (24.1 X 26.7 X 10.2 CM)
CREAMER, 7 X 8¼ X 2¾ INCHES (17.8 X 21 X 7 CM)
SUGAR BOWL, 5 X 5 X 2½ INCHES (12.7 X 12.7 X 6.4 CM)

Sterling silver, acrylic; textured, constructed, die formed

PHOTO BY ARTIST

Susan Myers

Disposable Series | 1997–2005

DIMENSIONS VARY

Silver-plated brass, bronze, copper,
sterling silver, found material; fabricated

PHOTOS BY JACK RAMSDALE

Timothy Lloyd

Kitano Fantasy Teapot | 2003

11½ X 12½ X 10 INCHES (29.2 X 31.8 X 25.4 CM)

Fine silver, antique coral; raised

PHOTO BY PETER LEE

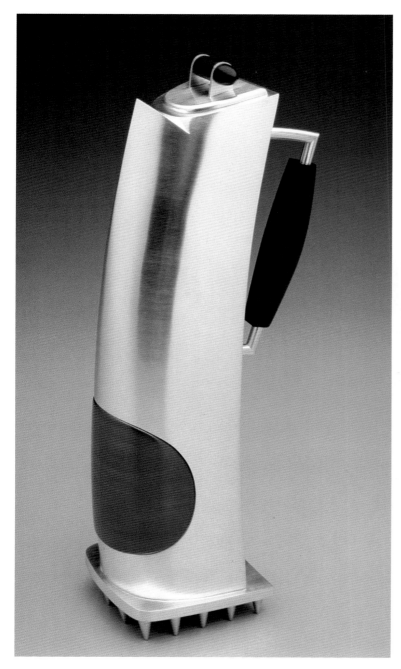

Tom Muir

Cycladic Figure Impregnated | 1987

10½ X 3 X 4 INCHES (26.7 X 7.6 X 10.2 CM)

Sterling silver, 18-karat yellow gold, copper; formed, fabricated, cast

PHOTOS BY ROB WHELESS

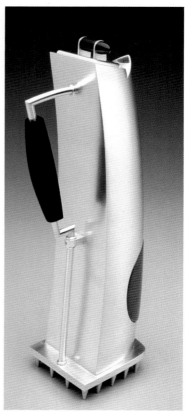

Phill Mason

Saturn-Saucer for a Future Medici | 1992

4 X 2½ X 2½ INCHES (10.2 X 6.4 X 6.4 CM)

Sterling silver, titanium, 18-karat gold, lapis, garnet; hollow fabricated, set

PHOTO BY UFFE SCHULZE

Quiescence *was made in 2002 during the invasion of Afghanistan by the allied forces. The lapis was mined in Afghanistan, and the design of the lid was inspired by Islamic ornament. The lid is hand pierced so that light can reflect through the lid onto the glass. The title means calm or peace.* —JB

John Blair

Quiescence | 2002

5 X 2½ INCHES (12.7 X 6.4 CM)

Sterling silver, lapis, glass; hand fabricated

PHOTO BY JOHN DEAN

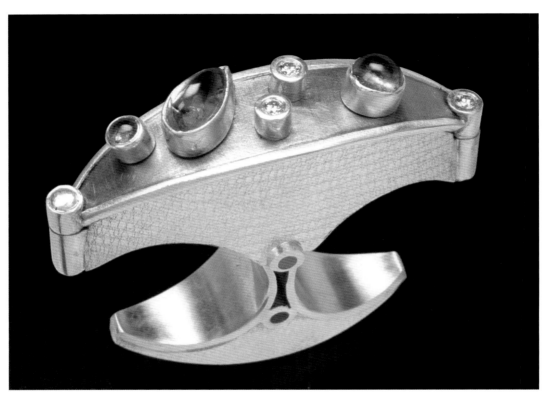

Intimate containers or vessels are appealing to me because they are diminutive and personal, often holding secrets and precious delights. —NA

Nanz Aalund

Empress (Toybox) | 2004

1⅝ X 1¾ X ½ INCH (4.1 X 4.5 X 1.3 CM)

Sterling silver, steel, magnets, diamonds, sapphire, emerald; fabricated

PHOTOS BY DOUG YAPLE

Ron Wilson

Wishing Cup | 2006

3⅝ X 2¼ INCHES (9.2 X 5.7 CM)

Sterling silver, metal, cactus amethyst quartz; die formed, sawed, filed, polished, welded, lapidary

PHOTO BY FORREST DOUD
COURTESY OF NOOR JEWELRY, SAN LUIS OBISPO, CALIFORNIA

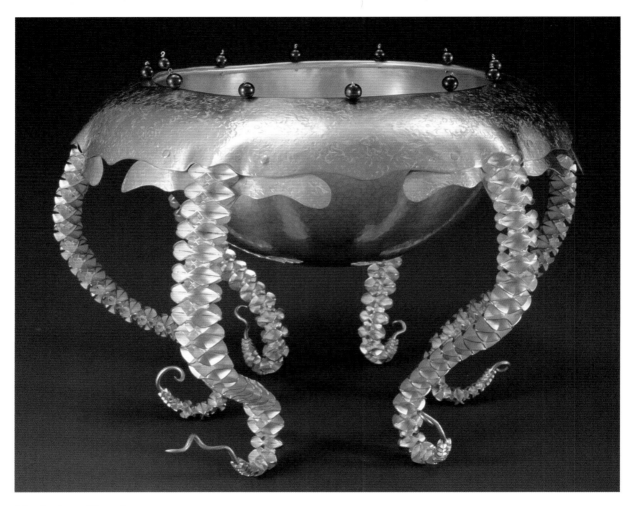

Linda Lee Shapiro

Sea Vessel | 2006

9 X 13 X 13 INCHES (22.9 X 33 X 33 CM)

Sterling silver, black pearls; raised, formed, fabricated

PHOTO BY ARTIST

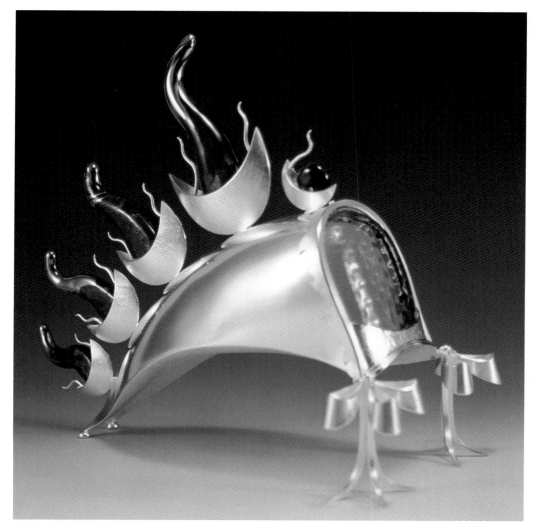

Helen Blythe-Hart

Silverfish: Holographic 3-D Animatecture Theater | 2004

12 X 4 X 12 INCHES (30.5 X 10.2 X 30.5 CM)
Sterling silver, glass; formed, forged, hollow constructed, blown

PHOTO BY ARTIST

Animatectures *are vessels which contain visions of the future. They're half bio-engineered animal and half architecture. I envision* Silverfish *as a holographic theater with projectors that fill the inside of the vessel with three-dimensional images. Hydraulic legs move the structure in sync with the "film."* —HBH

Jun Park

Devil Inside | 2006

6½ X 3 X 4 INCHES (16.5 X 7.6 X 10.2 CM)

Copper, brass, silver; forged, chased, cast, oxidized

PHOTO BY MYUNG-WOOK HUH, MUNCH STUDIO

Miel-Margarita Paredes

Octopus Teapot | 2005

8½ X 15 X 16 INCHES (21.6 X 38.1 X 40.6 CM)

Copper, sterling silver; raised, anticlastic forming, chased,
soldered

PHOTO BY STEPHEN FUNK
COLLECTION OF SONNY AND GLORIA KAMM

Miel-Margarita Paredes

Preening Teapot | 2005

10 X 6 X 12 INCHES (25.4 X 15.2 X 30.5 CM)

Copper, steel, sterling silver; raised, chased, forged, welded

PHOTO BY STEPHEN FUNK

Robin Kraft

Throat Soothers | 1999

8 X 8 X 8 INCHES (20.3 X 20.3 X 20.3 CM)

Sterling silver, patina; die formed, fabricated, cast

David A. Huang
Illusory Separation #313 | 2004

29 X 9½ X 9½ INCHES (73.7 X 24.1 X 24.1 CM)

Copper, patina; raised, chased

PHOTOS BY ARTIST

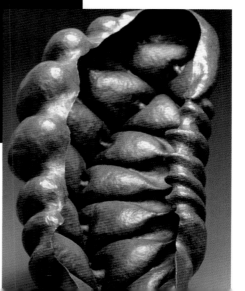

Sean Macmillan
Untitled Table Piece | 2003

28 X 12 X 12 INCHES (71.1 X 30.5 X 30.5 CM)
Copper, patina; hammer formed
PHOTOS BY ARTIST

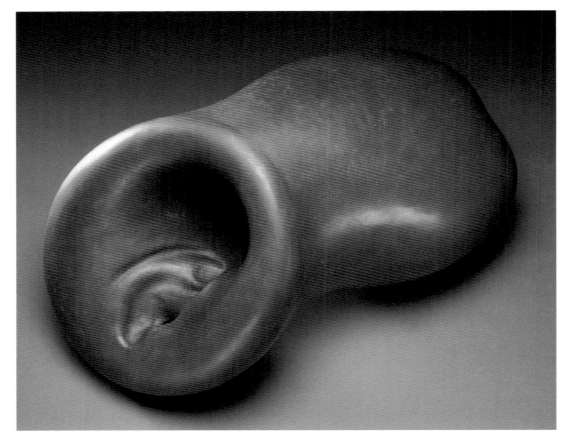

His-Hsia Yang

Ear Chamber | 2000

7½ X 8⁴/₅ X 15¾ INCHES (19 X 22.4 X 40 CM)

Copper; raised

PHOTO BY KUN-LUNG, TSAI

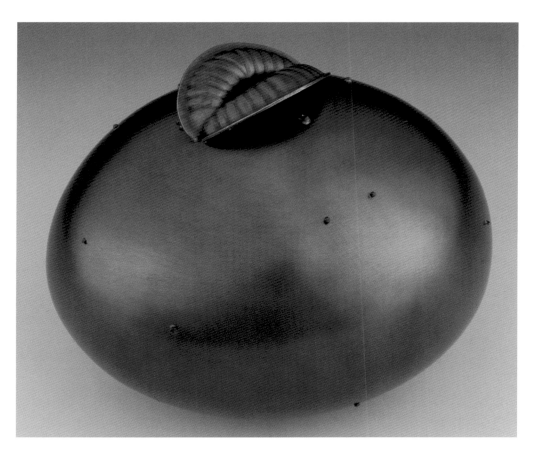

Susan R. Ewing

Laughable Loves: Kiss Vessel | 2004

6 X 6 X 6 INCHES (15.2 X 15.2 X 15.2 CM)

Bronze, Bohemian garnets, silver, patina; cast, fabricated

PHOTOS BY JEFFREY SABO

Maegan E. Crowley

Eye Bowl | 2003

6 X 13 X 14 INCHES (15.2 X 33 X 35.6 CM)

Steel; chased, forged, fabricated

PHOTO BY DOMINIC EPISCIPO

Carol K. Sakihara

Visceral Vessel | 2000

8½ X 8½ X 3¾ INCHES (21.6 X 21.6 X 9.5 CM)

Copper, liver of sulfur; raised, formed

PHOTO BY ARTIST

Tan-Chi Dandy Chao

Letters | 2001

3½ X 4¹³/₁₆ X 4¹³/₁₆ INCHES (8.9 X 12.2 X 12.2 CM)
Copper, patina; raised, photoetched
PHOTOS BY ARTIST

Seung-Hyun Lee
Sprouted | 2006

2½ X 3 X 4 INCHES (6.4 X 7.6 X 10.2 CM)
Copper, sterling silver, gold leaf; raised
PHOTOS BY MARUKO NARIAKI

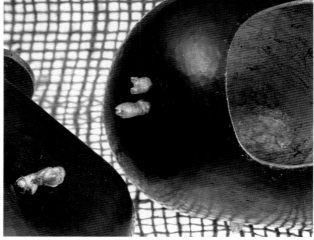

Alex Drummer

Untitled | 2006

7 X 12 X 12 INCHES (17.8 X 30.5 X 30.5 CM)

Railroad stakes; welded

PHOTO BY ARTIST

Yung-ling Tseng

Clone Container Series - Conjoined Quintuplets | 2005

4¾ X 12¾ X 1½ INCHES (12 X 32.4 X 3.8 CM)

Pewter; die formed, fabricated

PHOTO BY ARTIST

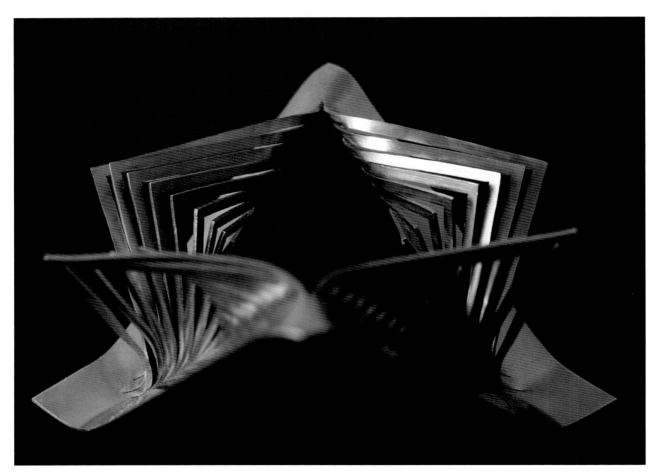

Yoshiko Yamamoto

Opened Vessel | 1989

4 X 6 X 6 INCHES (10.2 X 15.2 X 15.2 CM)

Bronze; sawed, formed

PHOTO BY ARTIST

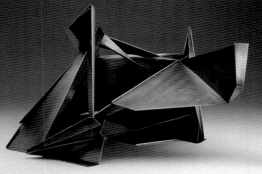

Ron Hinton

Buttress | 1992

12 X 12 X 16 INCHES (30.5 X 30.5 X 40.6 CM)

Bronze, copper; computer-generated drawing, photoetched, formed, fabricated

PHOTOS BY JON BLUMB

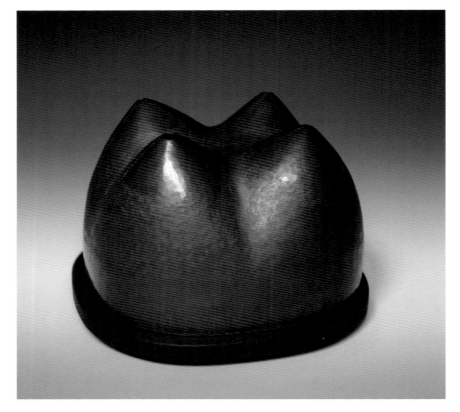

Cóilín O'Dubhghaill

Incense Burner | 2003

5½ X 4 X 4 INCHES (14 X 10.2 X 10.2 CM)

Copper, silver, iron, Niiro patina; raised, welded

PHOTO BY ARTIST

Sun Kyoung Kim

Mother's Love, 2001

5 X 19 X 3½ INCHES (12.7 X 48.3 X 8.9 CM)

Copper, silver; fabricated, cold connected

PHOTO BY ARTIST

Robyn Nichols

Thatch Palm Bowl | 2004

2¾ X 5 X 4 INCHES (7 X 12.7 X 10.2 CM)

Sterling silver; fabricated, chased, repoussé,
raised, forged, polished

PHOTO BY HOLLIS OFFICER

Peter Verburg

Untitled | 2005

LEFT, 1½ X 7 X 1½ INCHES (3.8 X 17.8 X 3.8 CM)
RIGHT, 2½ X 5½ X 2½ INCHES (6.4 X 14 X 6.4 CM)

Sterling silver; constructed, soldered

PHOTO BY ARTIST

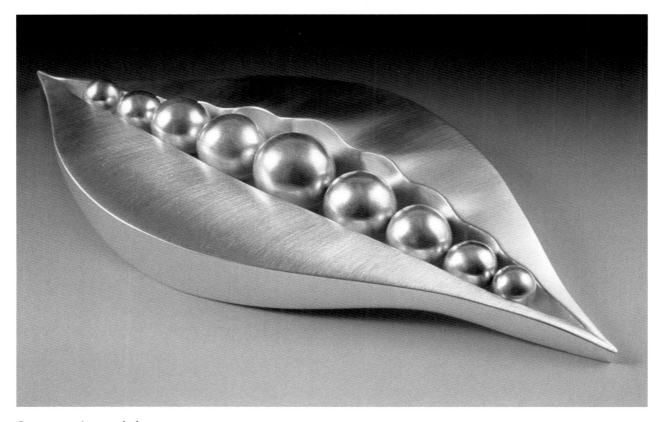

Suzanne Amendolara

Releasing Anxiety, Worry Beads | 2005

2 X 8 X 5 INCHES (5.1 X 20.3 X 12.7 CM)

Sterling silver; formed, fabricated

PHOTO BY ARTIST

Sputnik *is a battery-operated lamp. Inside the hollow ball are small LED lights that reflect into the polished silver. The position of the lamp can be changed.* —JM

Jan Matthesius
Sputnik | 2004

10 X 10 X 8 INCHES (25.4 X 25.4 X 20.3 CM)
Sterling silver, electronics; raised
PHOTO BY ROB GLASTRA

Sara Washbush

The Parting Glass: Union Cups | 2005

6¼ X 5½ X 3¼ INCHES (15.9 X 14 X 8.3 CM)

Silicon, bronze, sterling silver, gold leaf;
raised, fabricated

PHOTOS BY ARTIST

◄ **Felicity Peters**

Bowl: Broken Dream Clouds | 1998

4 X 5½ X 4½ INCHES (10.2 X 14 X 11.4 CM)
Sterling silver, 24-karat gold; folded, constructed, kum boo
PHOTO BY VICTOR FRANCE

▼ **Wanjin Kim**

Male & Female II | 2005

EACH, 3 X 4 X 4 INCHES (7.6 X 10.2 X 10.2 CM)
Fine silver; raised, forged, fabricated, kum boo
PHOTO BY DAVID TERAO

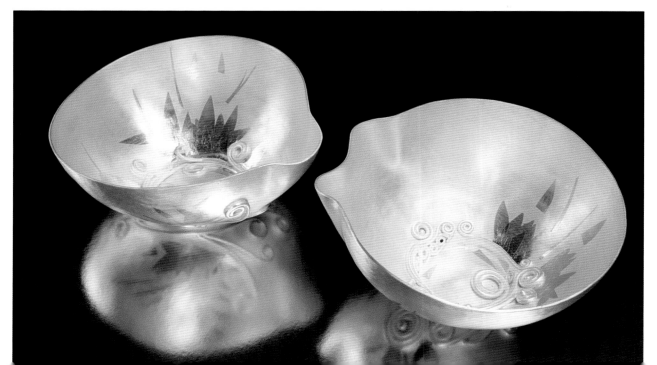

Momoko Okada

Wind Incense Burner | 2006

9 X 8 X 8 INCHES (22.9 X 20.3 X 20.3 CM)

Silver, gold, shakudo; raised, spun, damascened, inlaid

PHOTO BY SHINANO

Kye-Yeon Son

Calming | 2006

4¾ X 18 X 5 INCHES (4.75 X 45.7 X 12.7 CM)

Sterling silver, 24-karat gold plate; fabricated, soldered

PHOTO BY PERRY JACKSON

Mark Herndon

For Captain Nathaniel York, Astronaut | 2006

3½ X 2¾ X 2¾ INCHES (8.9 X 7 X 7 CM)

Sterling silver, copper; mokume gane

PHOTOS BY ARTIST

Ji Hoon Choi

Eternity | 2005

8 X 8 X 5 INCHES (20.3 X 20.3 X 12.7 CM)
Titanium, sterling silver, steel; anodized, inlaid, die formed

PHOTOS BY KWANG-CHOON PARK, KC STUDIO

Gordon K. Uyehara

Ceremonial Illumination Vessel | 2006

2½ X 3 X 3 INCHES (6.4 X 7.6 X 7.6 CM)

Silver clay

PHOTO BY ROBERT DIAMANTE

Lilyana Bekic

Tempted | 2005

5⅛ X 5⅛ X 5⅛ INCHES (13 X 13 X 13 CM)

Fine silver, ziricote, sterling silver, snakeskin, polymer clay,
ribbon; raised, lathe turned, die formed, fabricated

PHOTO BY ARTIST

Kelly Severtson

Untitled Sugar Bowl | 2006

3 X 3 X 3 INCHES (7.6 X 7.6 X 7.6 CM)

Silver, copper; mokume gane

PHOTO BY GEOFF SEBO

Tedd R. McDonah

Double-Wall Tea Cup | 1999

6½ X 4 X 4 INCHES (16.5 X 10.2 X 10.2 CM)

Sterling silver, copper; diffusion-bonded mokume gane, angle raised, anticlastic raising, soldered, screwed

PHOTO BY ALAN MCCOY
PRIVATE COLLECTION

Joy Stember

Kiddush Cup | 2004

6 X 7 X 7 INCHES (15.2 X 17.8 X 17.8 CM)

Bronze, aluminum; cast

PHOTO BY ARTIST

Robert Coogan

Sake Cup | 2005

6 X 2 X 2 INCHES (15.2 X 5.1 X 5.1 CM)

Copper, silver, green onyx; mokume gane, raised, bolted, fused

PHOTO BY ARTIST

Rob Jackson

Scopa Cups | 2000

EACH, 14 X 5 X 5 INCHES (35.6 X 12.7 X 12.7 CM)

Copper, silver, brass, tin; married metal, fabricated, chased, engraved, tinned

PHOTO BY ARTIST

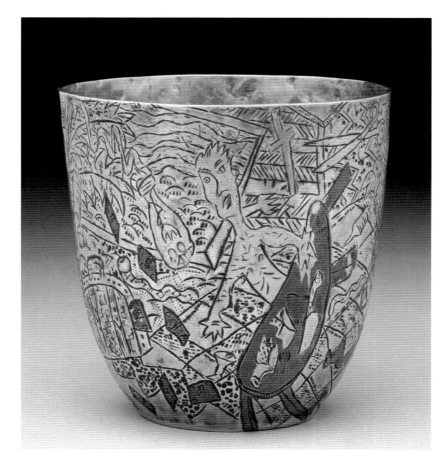

Louise Norrell

Party Cup | 1998

3½ X 3 INCHES (8.9 X 7.6 CM)

Fine silver, bronze, 14-karat gold, sterling silver; raised, appliqué soldered and hammered inlay, chased

PHOTO BY WALKER MONTGOMERY

Linda K. Darty

Treetop Series—
Pines and Ferns | 2006

11 X 6 X 6 INCHES (27.9 X 15.2 X 15.2 CM)

Sterling silver, fine silver, enamel, copper; etched, sifted, champlevé, fabricated

PHOTO BY ARTIST

Lin Stanionis

Eden of Eros | 1993

8 X 2 X 2 INCHES (20.3 X 5.1 X 5.1 CM)

Sterling silver, copper, Micarta, acrylic, parcel gilt, lacquers; carved, cast, formed, constructed

PHOTO BY JON BLUMB

Marian Slepian

Wedding Wine Cup | 2005

5 ½ X 3 INCHES (14 X 7.6 CM)

Fine silver, sterling silver, enamel, gold foil; spun, cloisonné, soldered, plated

PHOTO BY JACK ABRAHAM
COURTESY OF CELEBRATIONS GALLERY, NEW YORK, NEW YORK

Albion Smith

Untitled | 2006

2¾ X 3½ X 3 INCHES (7 X 8.9 X 7.6 CM)

Sterling silver, 18-karat gold, quartz, ruby, amethyst, enamel; pierced overlay, torch fired

PHOTO BY PAUL SCHRAUB

Judy Stone

Burnt Offering XIX | 2006

6 X 8½ X 6 INCHES (15.2 X 21.6 X 15.2 CM)

Copper, enamel, silver foil; spun, cut, riveted, sewn, sgraffito, limoges

PHOTO BY DOUG YAPLE

Tamar De Vries Winter

Ceremonial Cup | 2004

2¼ X 2¾ X 2¾ INCHES (5.7 X 7 X 7 CM)

Sterling silver, enamel; spun, engraved, champlevé

PHOTO BY PETER MENNIM

Harlan W. Butt

Earth Beneath Our Feet: Colorado Horizon #2 | 2006

6½ X 5 X 5 INCHES (16.5 X 12.7 X 12.7 CM)

Silver, enamel; raised, cloisonné, etched, cast, fabricated

PHOTO BY RAFAEL MOLINA

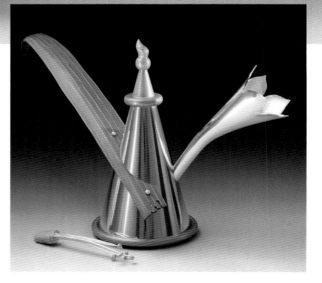

Kee-ho Yuen
Untitled | 2004

13½ X 4¼ X 7¼ INCHES (33 X 10.8 X 18.4 CM)

Gold, silver, aluminum, cork; fabricated, anodized

PHOTOS BY ARTIST
COLLECTION OF SONNY KAMM

Gina Westergard

Back to the Garden
(Funerary Urn) | 2003

39 X 17 X 17 INCHES (99.1 X 43.2 X 43.2 CM)

Copper, gold leaf, palladium leaf,
enamel paint, glass

PHOTOS BY ROBERT HICKERSON

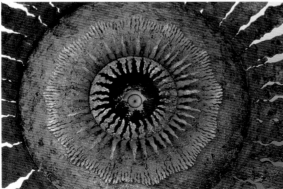

Helen Shirk

Clarice's Fancy | 2004

11 X 10 X 8 INCHES (27.9 X 25.4 X 20.3 CM)

Copper, patina, colored pencil; formed, fabricated

PHOTO BY ARTIST

Maggie Yi-Shin Liu

Heaven/Earth (Heaven) | 2002

4 X 10 X 10 INCHES (10.2 X 25.4 X 25.4 CM)

Copper, patina; raised, etched

PHOTOS BY KATHLEEN BROWNE

Louise Rauh

Early Autumn | 2005

7 X 14 X 14 INCHES (17.8 X 35.6 X 35.6 CM)
Aluminum, acrylic ink; spun, etched
PHOTO BY ARTIST

I keep going back to aluminum. As a metal artist, I find a singular beauty in this material most commonly associated with cooking utensils and the aerospace industry. The lightness and clean, white surface of the metal provide me with a nearly perfect canvas to work in three dimensions. Life in transformation, and the forces of nature with inevitable growth, deterioration, and regeneration are articulated as seasons and situations pass. Working with several layers of color on a deeply etched or manually textured surface, I attempt to narrow the perception of delicacy and durability. My intention is to convey a visual impression of fragility grounded in the inherent strength of the materials used. —LR

Thomas Mann

Patina Tea Vessels | 1994

16½ X 17 X 6 INCHES (41.9 X 43.2 X 15.2 CM)

Brass, bronze, patina; fabricated

PHOTO BY GERARD PERRONE

My intention is to make the funerary urn an object that initiates a celebration of a life. Rich surfaces and vibrant colors evoke joy. The minimal, stately exterior of each urn gradually leads to more detailed and recessed interior space. Nestled within each lid is an element that awaits discovery, representing new growth and renewal. —GW

Gina Westergard
Eclipse (Funerary Urn) | 2005

8¼ X 16½ X 16½ INCHES (21 X 41.9 X 41.9 CM)

Copper, gold leaf, palladium leaf, enamel paint, chrysoprase

PHOTOS BY ROBERT HICKERSON

Patricia A. Nelson

Flagellate | 2005

10 X 14 X 14 INCHES (25.4 X 35.6 X 35.6 CM)

Copper, silver, enamel, ebonized oak; forged, formed, constructed

PHOTO BY SERENA NANCARROW

Linda K. Darty

Garden Candlestick Trio | 2006

TALLEST, 7 X 6 X 6 INCHES (17.8 X 15.2 X 15.2 CM)

Copper, enamel; fabricated, sifted

PHOTO BY ARTIST

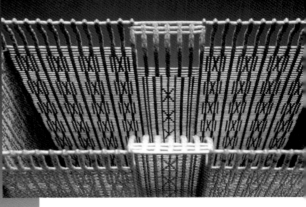

Dennis Nahabetian

*Vessel #63
(Empire State)* | 2003

14 X 8 X 3½ INCHES (35.6 X 20.3 X 8.9 CM)

Copper, bronze, 24-karat gold,
patina, polychrome

PHOTOS BY ARTIST

Bruce Paul Gaber

Bud Vase | 2005

5¼ X 1¼ X 1¼ INCHES (13.3 X 3.2 X 3.2 CM)

Pewter; hand formed

PHOTO BY ARTIST

Jon Ryan

Untitled | 2006

4¾ X 5 X 5 INCHES (12 X 12.7 X 12.7 CM)

Titanium; pierced, folded, anodized

PHOTO BY ARTIST

David Huycke

Marble Bowl | 2006

6 X 6½ X 6½ INCHES (15.2 X 16.5 X 16.5 CM)

Sterling silver, patina; granulation

PHOTO BY ARTIST

Jon Michael Route

Pewter Coil Pot | 2005

8¼ X 6½ X 6½ INCHES (21 X 16.5 X 16.5 CM)

Pewter; stretched, fabricated

PHOTO BY DEB ROUTE

Jessica Benzaquen

Container for a Dream | 2004

6 X 3 X 2 INCHES (15.2 X 7.6 X 5.1 CM)

Sterling silver, fine silver; raised, chased, repoussé, fabricated

PHOTOS BY ARTIST

Wayne Jay

Last Stop | 2004

5 X 4½ X 4½ INCHES (12.7 X 11.4 X 11.4 CM)

Steel; forged, fold formed, welded, riveted, waxed firescale finish

PHOTO BY ARTIST

Sara Krempel

Covered Bowl | 1985

3½ X 4½ X 4½ INCHES (8.9 X 11.4 X 11.4 CM)

Pewter, copper; raised, chased, repoussé, fabricated

PHOTOS BY ARTIST

Leslie Matthews

Scapula Vessel | 2005

3³/₁₆ X 3½ X 3³/₁₆ INCHES (8 X 9 X 8 CM)
Sterling silver, black patina
PHOTO BY GRANT HANCOCK

Leslie Matthews

Scapula Vessels | 2005

WHITE, 3³/₁₆ X 3³/₁₆ X 2¾ INCHES (8 X 8 X 7 CM)
BLACK, 6 X 6 X ¹⁵/₁₆ INCH (15 X 15 X 2.5 CM)
Sterling silver, black patina
PHOTO BY GRANT HANCOCK

Julie Blyfield

Flourish Vessel Series | 2005

6⁷/₈ X 2³/₁₆ X 2³/₁₆ INCHES (17.5 X 5.5 X 5.5 CM)

Pure silver, copper; oxidized, wax finish

PHOTOS BY GRANT HANCOCK
COURTESY OF GALLERY FUNAKI, MELBOURNE, AUSTRALIA

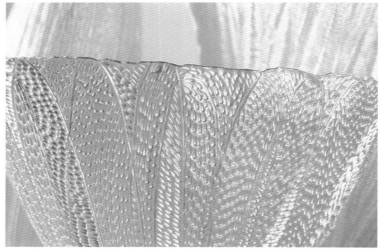

Sally Marsland

Domestic Vessels | 1998

TALLEST, 24 X 3 X 3 INCHES (61 X 7.6 X 7.6 CM)

Aluminum, sterling silver, found wooden handles; anodized, lathe turned, raised, assembled, cast

PHOTO BY ARTIST

Bridget Kennedy

Still Life with Gold Vessel | 2005

LARGEST, 4 X 3¼ X 3¼ INCHES (10.2 X 8.3 X 8.3 CM)

Fine silver, sterling silver, spinning silver, copper, gilding
metal, fine gold, enamel, graphite; raised

PHOTO BY ROSS BUCHANAN

June Jasen

*The Golden Path That the Dragonflies in
Kaos Took to Find Their Way* | 2006

8 X 4¾ X 7½ INCHES (20.3 X 12 X 19 CM)

Enamel, copper cloth, 24-karat gold leaf; transferred,
brass edged, fused

PHOTO BY ARTIST

Gary Kim Harris

Bee Jewelry Box | 2006

2¾ X 2¾ INCHES (7 X 7 CM)

Silver, bronze; lost wax cast

PHOTO BY CAROL HARRIS

Barbara Minor
Untitled | 2005

4¼ X 4 X 4 INCHES (10.8 X 10.2 X 10.2 CM)

Glass, enamel, fine silver, 24-karat gold foil, copper, matte onyx, sterling silver; raised, fabricated

PHOTOS BY RALPH GABRINER

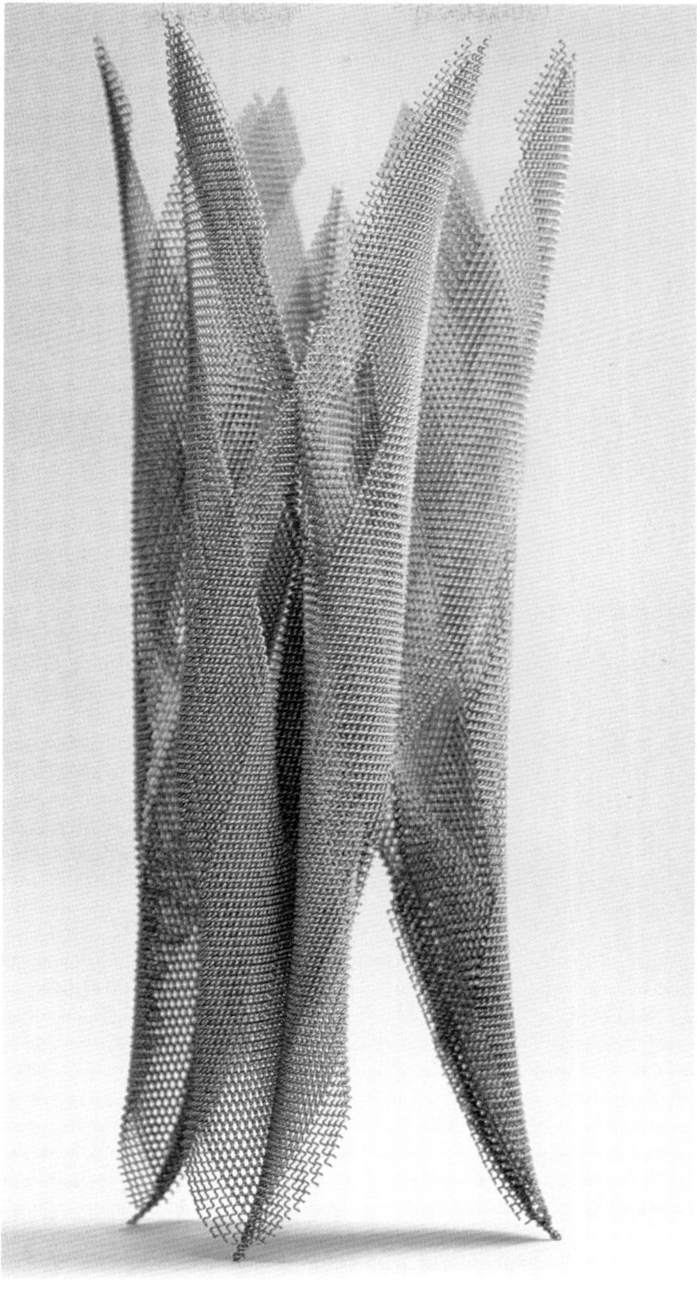

Alexandru Usineviciu

Flames | 2005

20½ X 8 X 8 INCHES (52.1 X 20.3 X 20.3 CM)
Brass wire; spiraled, interlinked
PHOTO BY ARTIST

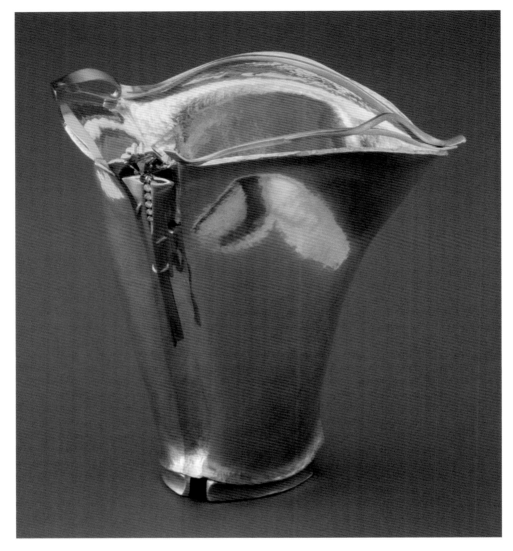

Linda M. Weiss

Hemerocallis Hybrid | 1998

6½ X 6¼ X 6¼ INCHES (16.5 X 15.9 X 15.9 CM)

18-karat gold, platinum, tourmaline, diamonds

PHOTO BY JOHN BRESSIE

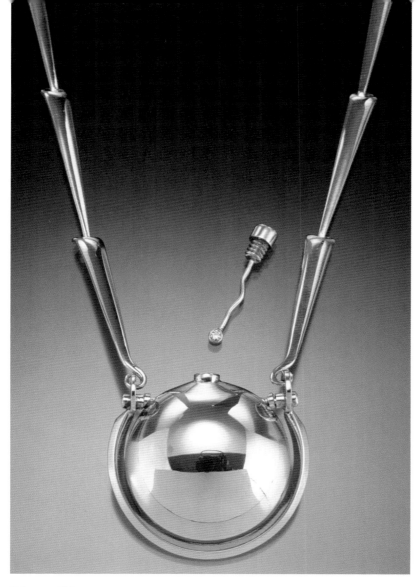

Wayne Werner

Circle of Life Chain | 1997

VESSEL, 1¼ X 1¼ X 1¼ INCHES (3.2 X 3.2 X 3.2 CM)
CHAIN, 22 INCHES (55.9 CM)

18-karat gold, 14-karat gold, diamonds; forged, hollow formed

PHOTO BY RALPH GABRINER

Tom Ferrero

Port Cups | 2006

EACH, 4 X 3 X 3 INCHES (10.2 X 7.6 X 7.6 CM)
Sterling silver, 18-karat gold, copper
PHOTO BY KEVIN MONTAGUE

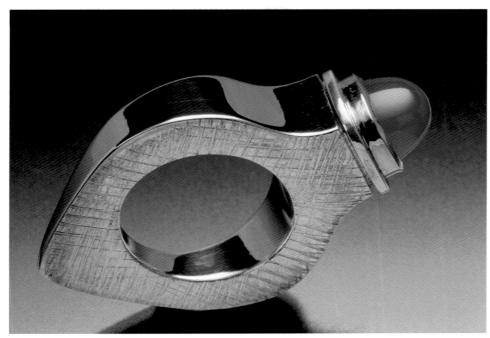

The profile of this ring is influenced by ancient Greek urns. —NA

Nanz Aalund

The Fool (an empty vessel) | 2004

1¾ X ½ X 1⅛ INCHES (4.5 X 1.3 X 2.8 CM)

14-karat rose gold, sterling silver, platinum, blue chalcedony; fabricated, hammered, bezel set

PHOTOS BY DOUG YAPLE

Barbara Bayne

Untitled Cups | 2001

4³/₈ X 2 X 2 INCHES (11.2 X 5.1 X 5.1 CM)
4 X 1⁷/₈ X 1⁷/₈ INCHES (10.2 X 4.7 X 4.7 CM)

18-karat gold, sterling silver; textured, die formed,
fabricated, oxidized

PHOTO BY DAVID RAMSEY

Andy Cooperman

Seymour's Cup | 2005

9 X 4 INCHES (22.9 X 10.2 CM)

Sterling silver, 18-karat gold, 24-karat gold plate, ruby;
raised, planished, fused, forged, fabricated

PHOTO BY DOUG YAPLE

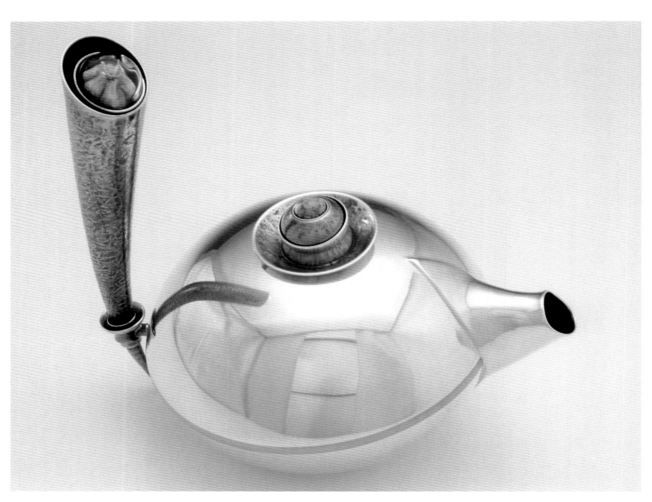

Angela Bubash

Reverence | 2005

6 X 4½ X 5½ INCHES (15.2 X 11.4 X 14 CM)

Sterling silver, copper, glass, garnet, nigella seeds and pods; forged, fabricated, die formed, raised

PHOTO BY TOM MILLS

The glass elements were treated with a sense of secrecy and discovery, especially when you remove the lid and find a large specimen beneath. —AB

Lilyana Bekic

Tea for Two | 1996

6 X 6 X 5¼ INCHES (15.2 X 15.2 X 13.3 CM)

Nickel silver, anodized aluminum; fabricated, lathe turned

PHOTO BY ARTIST

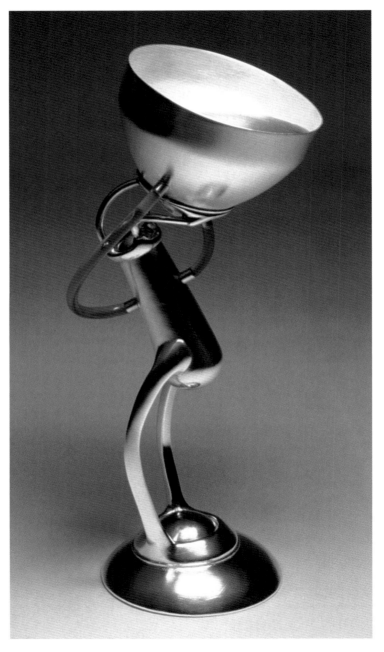

Kirk Lang

Chalice | 2000

11 X 4 X 4 INCHES (27.9 X 10.2 X 10.2 CM)

Sterling silver, PVC tubing

PHOTO BY MATTHEW HOLLERN

Oliver Smith

Pump Dispenser #2 | 2000

8 X 6 X 15 INCHES (20.3 X 15.2 X 38.1 X CM)

Anodized aluminum, stainless steel, Delrin, rubber; hammered

PHOTO BY SEAN BOOTH

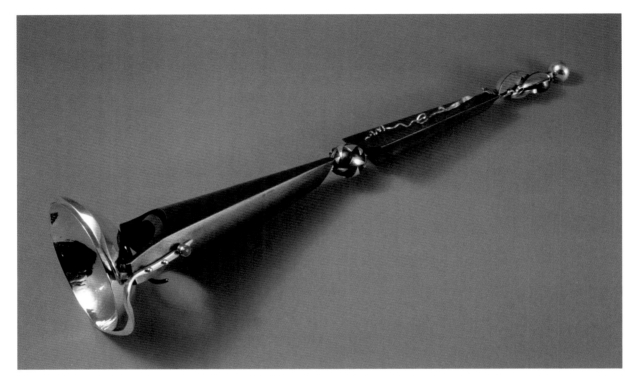

Sandra Dovberg

Wine Tasting Vessel | 1999

14⅛ X 3½ X 3½ INCHES (35.6 X 8.9 X 8.9 CM)

Brass, sterling silver, copper, chrysocolla; hollow formed, raised, forged, soldered, tap and die, threaded, cold connected

PHOTO BY ARTIST

I wanted to make an outlandish vessel. My departure point was a wine taster's humble tasting cup that is worn around the neck. I placed it at the top of a scepter-like structure to impart a sense of royalty and the organic feel of fruit at the end of a stalk. Along the large brass hollowforms are smaller hollowforms reminiscent of grapes and forged wires reminiscent of vines. —SD

This wearable perfume bottle represents an alternative method of 'wearing' perfume. —PM

Phill Mason

Bangle-Bottle | 2005

2½ X 2½ X ¼ INCH (6.4 X 6.4 X 0.6 CM)

Sterling silver, 18-karat gold, threaded stopper, iron pyrites; hollow fabricated

PHOTO BY UFFE SCHULZE

Fred Fenster
Sabbath Candlesticks | 1997

EACH, 7½ X 3 INCHES (19 X 7.6 CM)
Sterling silver; raised, constructed
PHOTO BY ARTIST

Marian Slepian

Bud Vase | 2004

8 X 2¾ INCHES (20.3 X 7 CM)

Sterling silver, fine silver, jade, enamel;
spun, soldered

PHOTO BY JACK ABRAHAM

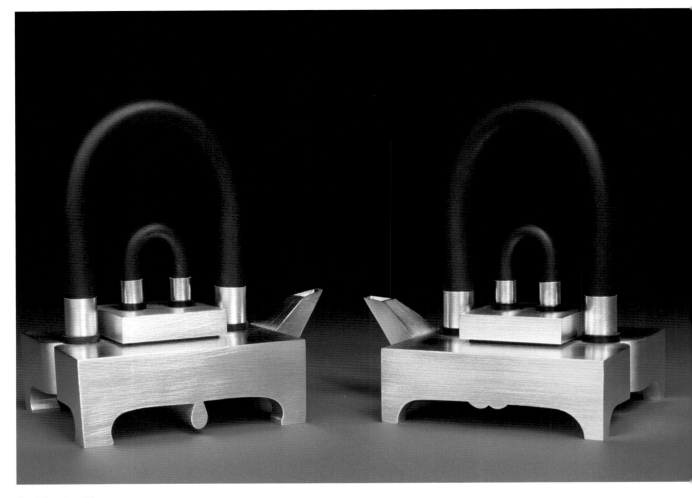

Robly A. Glover

Flirtation Tea Servers | 2002

EACH, 6 X 4 X 4 INCHES (15.2 X 10.2 X 10.2 CM)

Sterling silver, rubber; constructed

PHOTO BY ARTIST
COURTESY OF SMITHSONIAN AMERICAN ART MUSEUM'S RENWICK GALLERY,
WASHINGTON, D.C.

John Kent Garrott

Espresso Server #1, #2, #3 | 2004

EACH, 4 X 8 X 2 INCHES (10.2 X 20.3 X 5.1 CM)

Sterling silver; fabricated

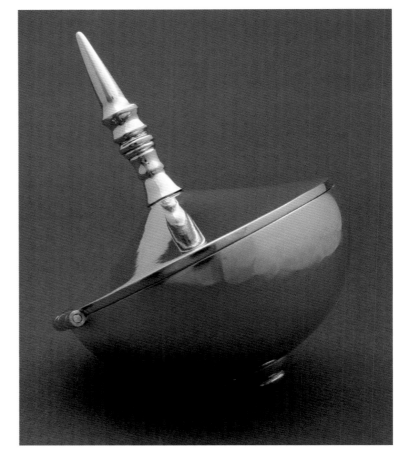

When closed, this is a spinning top toy. Opened, it reveals an elegant container for a special piece of jewelry, especially a ring, which can easily fit over the rose quartz tongue. —SD

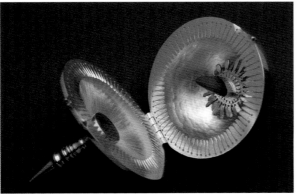

Sandra Dovberg
Keeper of the Ring | 1999

3³/₁₆ X 2⁵/₁₆ X 2⁵/₁₆ INCHES (8.1 X 5.9 X 5.9 CM)

Sterling silver, ruby in zoisite, frosted rose quartz tongue; sandcast, raised, soldered, constructed

PHOTOS BY ARTIST

The idea for this piece comes from a childhood memory of setting up mushrooms on paper overnight and creating a spore print that copied the gills from the underside of the mushroom. The spores drop from the gill structure, inspiring the idea of mushroom as container and shaker. The silver stem and gill structure is removed to fill the vessel, the lid is replaced, and the spices are shaken out through slots, creating a linear pattern. —HB

Heather Bayless

Spore Shaker | 2006

3½ X 2¾ X 2¾ INCHES (8.9 X 7 X 7 CM)

Sterling silver; raised, hand fabricated

PHOTO BY KWANG-CHOON PARK, KC STUDIO

Todd Jeffrey Ellis

Beatrice-Elizabeth | 2004

8 X 5 X 3 INCHES (20.3 X 12.7 X 7.6 CM)

Sterling silver, rubies, sapphires, garnet; raised, chased, repoussé

PHOTO BY ARTIST

Gail Ralston

Organic Cups | 2001

9½ X 1½ X 1¾ INCHES (24.1 X 3.8 X 4.4 CM)

Sterling silver, nickel; roller printed, die formed, fabricated

PHOTO BY SARAH PERKINS

Jessica S. Mohl

Burgeoning | 2006

6½ X 3¼ X 2½ INCHES (16.5 X 8.3 X 6.4 CM)

Sterling silver; raised, formed, fold formed, soldered

PHOTO BY ARTIST

Ewa Doerenkamp

Spiky-bowls | 1999

38 X 21¾ X 15 INCHES (96 X 55 X 38 CM)

Copper, gilding metal, sterling silver; raised, mounted

PHOTO BY ARTIST

Cynthia Lewis

Twister | 2003

10½ X 4 X 4 INCHES (26.7 X 10.2 X 10.2 CM)

Bronze, sterling silver, 24-karat gold, glass, amethyst; unique cast, soldered, heavy deposition plated, flameworked, bezel set

PHOTO BY ARTIST
COLLECTION OF DARCY SETY

Courtney L. Green

122 Days | 2004

5 X 7 X 10 INCHES (12.7 X 17.8 X 25.4 CM)

Lead, plaster

PHOTO BY HANS-JURGEN BERGMANN

◀ **Bryan Scott Petersen**

Penland World | 2004

13 X 10 X 10 INCHES (33 X 25.4 X 25.4 CM)

Copper, brass, machine fasteners; fold formed, sunk, raised, fused, embossed, soldered

PHOTO BY ARTIST

▼ **Kathleen Janzen**

Fragmented Vessel | 2005

5 X 16 X 17 INCHES (12.7 X 40.6 X 43.2 CM)

Steel; torch cut, welded

PHOTO BY NOEL BEGIN

Lu Heintz

Untitled | 2005

6 X 12 X 12 INCHES (15.2 X 30.5 X 30.5 CM)

Steel; riveted, forged, pressed

PHOTO BY KAREN PHILIPPI

◀ **Annette Zey**

Bowl | 2005

6 X 7½ INCHES (15.2 X 19 CM)
Copper, black patina, 24-karat gold leaf; soldered
PHOTO BY ARTIST

▼ **Molly Groom Alter**

Steel Bowl | 2005

7 X 12 X 14 INCHES (17.8 X 30.5 X 35.6 CM)
Steel; forged, heat formed, riveted
PHOTO BY ARTIST

Catherine H. Grisez
Nesting; Emergence | 2003

3 X 10¼ X 10¼ INCHES (7.6 X 26 X 26 CM)

Brass, bronze, copper, sterling silver; raised, cast, electroformed, fabricated

PHOTOS BY DOUG YAPLE

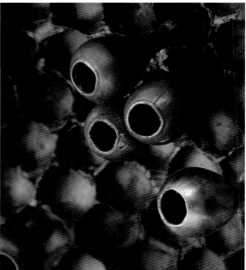

Danielle Crissman

Droplet, 2001

5 X 6 X 4½ INCHES (12.7 X 15.2 X 11.4 CM)

Copper; raised, chased, repoussé

PHOTO BY ERICKA CRISSMAN, WIRED IMAGES
COLLECTION OF MR. AND MRS. ANDRUS

Michelle Ritter

Remembrance | 2002

14 X 4 X 4 INCHES (35.6 X 10.2 X 10.2 CM)

Copper, brass, nickel silver, patina;
raised, formed, soldered

PHOTO BY HELEN SHIRK

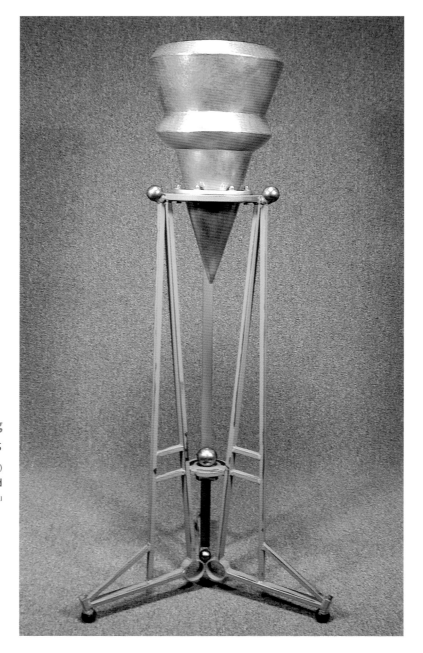

Dale Wedig

Science Project | 2005

58 X 24 X 24 INCHES (147.3 X 61 X 61 CM)

Copper, steel; raised, fabricated

PHOTO BY MICHAEL CINELLI

Natasha Overholtzer

Triple Tinge of Tension with Holy Hue | 2006

9¼ X 3 X 3 INCHES (23.5 X 7.6 X 7.6 CM)

Copper; electroformed, fabricated

PHOTO BY ARTIST

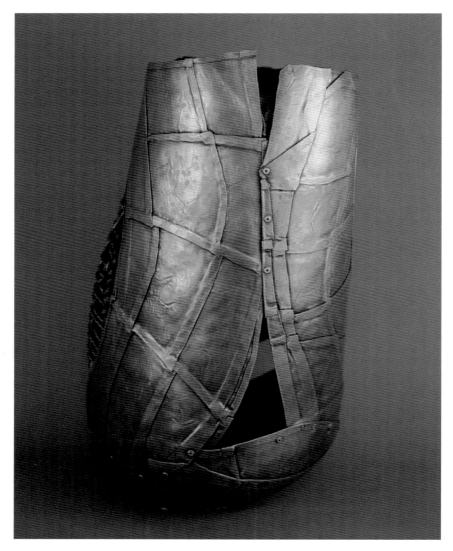

Elliott Pujol

Bryce | 1989

21 X 12 INCHES (53.3 X 30.5 CM)

Copper, bronze

PHOTO BY PHOTOGRAPHICS
COLLECTION OF TOM TYLER

Corey Ackelmire
Oval Quilted Bowl Pair | 2006
LARGEST, 3 X 15 X 9 INCHES (7.6 X 38.1 X 22.9 CM)
Copper, patina; raised, stamped, pierced

Dong Hyun Kim

Untitled Vessel | 2005

4½ X 10 X 5½ INCHES (11.4 X 25.4 X 14 CM)

Copper, patina; hammered, hand fabricated

PHOTO BY MUNCH STUDIO
COLLECTION OF DIE NEVE SAMMLUNG, GERMANY

James Viste

Stones (break a plow) | 2005

10 X 10 X 10 INCHES (25.4 X 25.4 X 25.4 CM)

Steel, copper, tin; die forged, fabricated

PHOTO BY ARTIST

John Tzelepis

Perpetual Motion #1 | 2006

7½ X 8 X 8 INCHES (19 X 20.3 X 20.3 CM)

Brass, stainless steel, rare earth magnets

PHOTO BY ARTIST

David Wagner

Teapot | 2005

6 X 5 X 7 INCHES (15.2 X 12.7 X 17.8 CM)

Copper; raised, fabricated

PHOTO BY MICHAEL BRAY

Becky I. Chader

Digging for Gold: A Reliquary for the Dandelion | 2006

9 X 8 X 8 INCHES (22.9 X 20.3 X 20.3 CM)

Copper, wood, glass, dandelion seeds; raised, fold formed, fabricated

PHOTO BY BECKY MCDONAH

Cappy Counard

To Live Wisely | 2005

4 X 1½ X 1³⁄₈ INCHES (10.2 X 3.8 X 3.5 CM)

14-karat gold, copper, acorn, spring; scored, folded, formed, fabricated

PHOTOS BY ARTIST
COURTESY OF THE HELEN DRUTT GALLERY,
PHILADELPHIA, PENNSYLVANIA

Tom Muir

Watercourse Teapot | 2003

12½ X 7¼ X 4 INCHES (31.8 X 18.4 X 10.2 CM)

Copper, brass, aluminum; formed, fabricated, chased, machined

PHOTOS BY TIM THAYER

Sadie Shu-Ping Wang

Copper Teapot with Cherry Tray | 2004

6½ X 6½ X 1½ INCHES (16.5 X 16.5 X 3.8 CM)

Sterling silver, copper, cherry wood, brass; hydraulic die formed, fabricated

PHOTO BY JOHN LUCAS

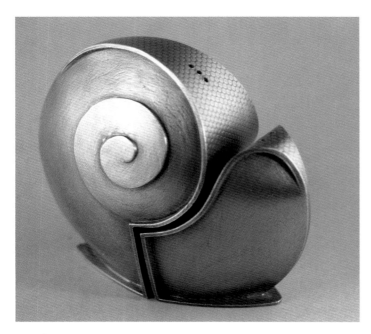

Fred Fenster

Salt and Pepper Shakers | 2003

4¾ X 2½ INCHES (12 X 6.4 CM)

Pewter; raised, constructed

PHOTO BY ARTIST

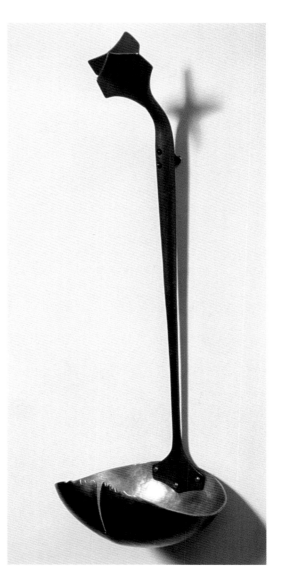

John J. Rais

Lights Out | 2004

24 X 8 X 7 INCHES (61 X 20.3 X 17.8 CM)

Steel, bronze, patina; forged, fabricated

PHOTO BY D. JAMES DEE
COLLECTION OF HARVEY AND FIONA FIEN

Jonathan Wahl

American Heritage Series II, Pitchers | 1997

EACH, 72 X 16 X 16 INCHES (182.9 X 40.6 X 40.6 CM)

Steel, tin, enamel paint

PHOTO BY PETER MERETSKY
COLLECTION OF THE MUSEUM OF ARTS & DESIGN,
NEW YORK, NEW YORK

Robert Griffith

Light Vessel-Torchiere | 2005

76 X 22 X 22 INCHES (193 X 55.9 X 55.9 CM)

Steel; spun, powder coated, fabricated

PHOTO BY LISA HINKLE MARIA
COLLECTION OF CESAR MUJAR

Chi Yu Fang

Cup | 2005

3¼ X 3¼ X 5¼ INCHES (8 X 8 X 13 CM)
Pewter; soldered, forged
PHOTOS BY CHUANG-SHENG TSAI

Matthew Hollern

Succulent Forms | 2001

16 X 5 X 4 INCHES (40.6 X 12.7 X 10.2 CM)
13 X 5 X 4 INCHES (33 X 12.7 X 10.2 CM)
10 X 5 X 4 INCHES (25.4 X 12.7 X 10.2 CM)

Pewter; fabricated

PHOTO BY ARTIST
COLLECTION OF SMITHSONIAN AMERICAN ART
MUSEUM'S RENWICK GALLERY, WASHINGTON, D.C.

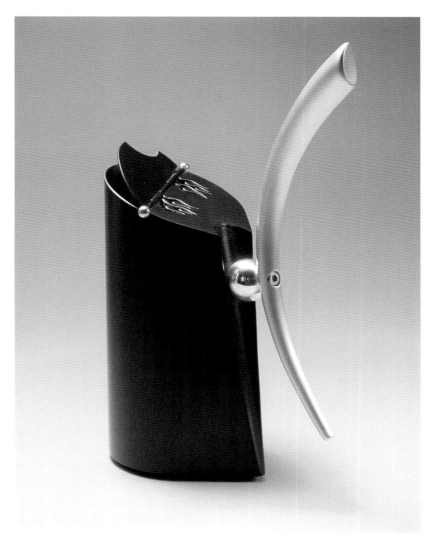

Jason Messier

Black Reaper | 2006

8½ X 3 X 5 INCHES (21.6 X 7.6 X 12.7 CM)

Stainless steel, aluminum; powder coated

PHOTO BY ARTIST

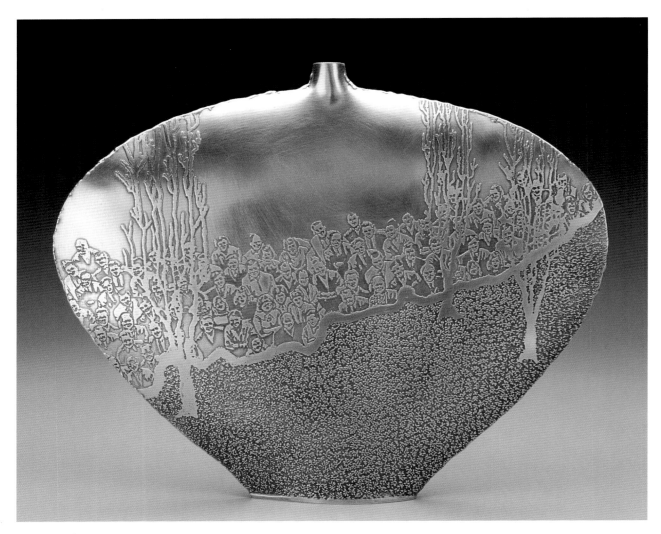

Claire Pfleger
Where Do We Fit? | 2002

8 X 10 X 1½ INCHES (20.3 X 25.4 X 3.8 CM)
Pewter, copper; fabricated, etched
PHOTO BY LARRY SANDERS

Casey Miller

Homage to Mondrian | 2006

5 X 5 X 6 INCHES (12.7 X 12.7 X 15.2 CM)

Copper, Delrin, acrylic gesso, prismacolor; formed, soldered

PHOTO BY HELEN SHIRK

Alexis Rae Archibald

A Process | 2004

4 X 6 X 4 INCHES (10.2 X 15.2 X 10.2 CM)

Copper, sterling silver, glass, beeswax; married metal,
raised, soldered, riveted, hinged

PHOTO BY ARTIST

Gina Westergard

Sogni D'Oro (Funerary Urn) | 2005

12 X 12 X 12 INCHES (30.5 X 30.5 X 30.5 CM)

Copper, silver, gold leaf, enamel paint, boulder opal

PHOTO BY ROBERT HICKERSON

Kristie Reiser

Bond | 2005

5½ X 3½ X 3½ INCHES (14 X 8.9 X 8.9 CM)

Pewter, brass, patina; raised, fabricated

PHOTO BY BILL LEMKE

Agnes Chwae

Night | 1993

4½ X 11 X 11 INCHES (11.4 X 27.9 X 27.9 CM)

Pewter, silver; hammered, fused, soldered

PHOTO BY JIM WILDEMAN
COLLECTION OF RUTHANNE BESSMAN

Thomas Mann

Kiddush Cup/Sanctify | 1998

CUP, 5 X 2½ X 2½ INCHES (12.7 X 6.4 X 6.4 CM)
HOLDER, 8 X 4 X 4 INCHES (20.3 X 10.2 X 10.2 CM)

Sterling silver, steel, patina; formed,
rusted, fabricated

PHOTO BY GERARD PERRONE

Pamela Morris Thomford

Valiant Duty (Tzdekah/Alms Box) | 2004

10 X 3 X 3 INCHES (25.4 X 7.6 X 7.6 CM)

Bronze, sterling silver, glass, mirrors; corrugated, die formed, raised, fabricated

PHOTO BY KEITH MEISER

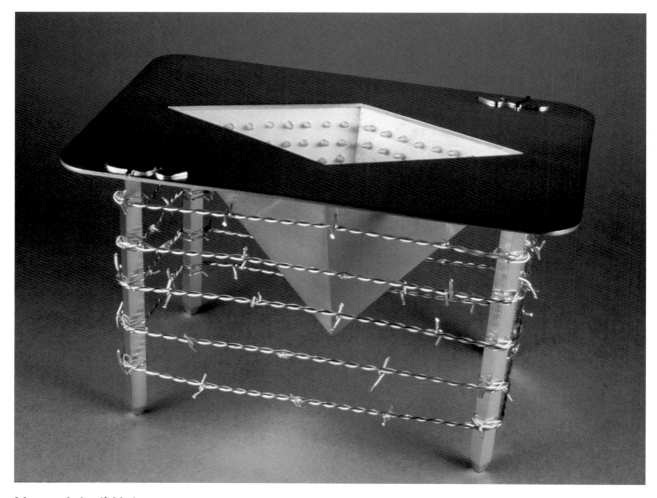

Munya Avigail Upin

Is She Really Your Best Bet? | 1985

3 X 4½ X 3¼ INCHES (7.6 X 11.4 X 8.3 CM)
Sterling silver, copper; fabricated
PHOTO BY ARTIST

Curtis K. LaFollette

Rust Belt Tea Strainer | 2006

5 X 4¼ X 6½ INCHES (12.7 X 10.8 X 16.5 CM)

Sterling silver, rosewood, brass, stainless steel, mild steel;
raised, fabricated

PHOTO BY BOB NASH

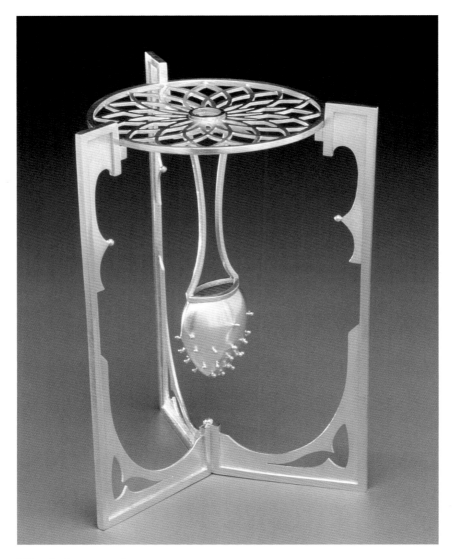

Nicole Jacquard

Dahlia Bud Vase | 2000

6 X 3½ X 3½ INCHES (15.2 X 8.9 X 8.9 CM)

Silver, 18-karat gold, brass; die formed, pierced, soldered, fabricated

PHOTO BY KEVIN MONTAGUE

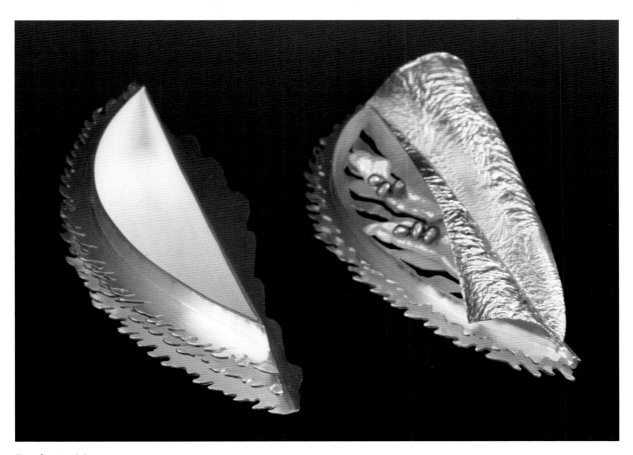

Paulette Myers

Voyage: Spirit Waters I | 2004

1½ X 4 X 1¾ INCHES (3.8 X 10.2 X 4.4 CM)

Sterling silver, pearls; fabricated, reticulated, formed

PHOTO BY ARTIST

Eduardo Rubio-Arzate

Perfume Bottle | 2003

4 X ¾ X 3¼ INCHES (10.2 X 1.9 X 8.3 CM)

Sterling silver, carnelian; fabricated, hollow formed

PHOTO BY ERICK SWANSON

Caro

Untitled | 2004

10½ X 4½ X 5½ INCHES (26.7 X 11.4 X 14 CM)
Silver, copper, nickel silver;
sunk, soldered
PHOTO BY KYE-YEON SON

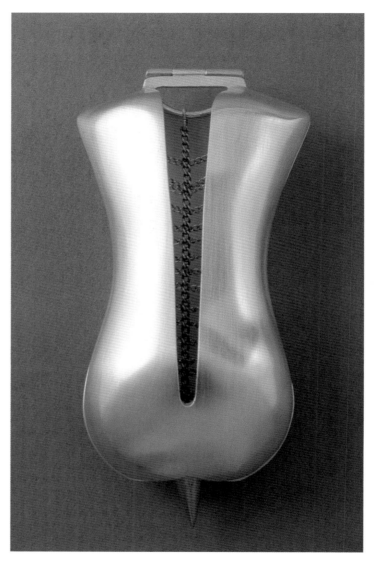

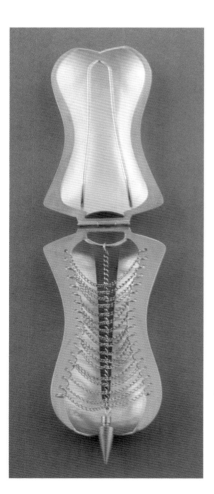

Thelma Coles

With the Flow | 2005

2½ X 1³⁄₈ X ¾ INCH (6.4 X 3.5 X 1.9 CM)

Silver, red brass; hydraulic pressed, constructed

PHOTOS BY ARTIST

Charleen Weidell
Benediction | 2000

7 X 14 X 7 INCHES (17.8 X 35.6 X 17.8 CM)
Sterling silver, enamel, glass beads; constructed
PHOTOS BY ARTIST

I play with stability and instability, as well as elegance and whimsy. —SK

Satomi Kawai

Tilting Container I | 2005

14¾ X 3 X 2 INCHES (37.5 X 7.6 X 5.1 CM)

Sterling silver, plastic; formed, soldered, cold connected

PHOTO BY ARTIST

Kee-Ho Yuen

Untitled | 2006

13½ X 5¼ X 7½ INCHES (34.3 X 13.3 X 19 CM)

Gold, silver, aluminum, brass, rock, laser printer ink, acrylic
paint, enamel paint; fabricated, anodized, image transfer

PHOTO BY ARTIST

Darlys Ewoldt

Contemplating the Shape of Water | 2006

7½ X 23 X 19 INCHES (18 X 58.4 X 48.3 CM)

Copper, patina; angle raised, formed, fabricated

PHOTO BY ARTIST

Louise Rauh

Blue Prairie | 2005

7 X 14 X 14 INCHES (17.8 X 35.6 X 35.6 CM)

Aluminum, acrylic ink; spun, etched

PHOTO BY ARTIST

Sarah Perkins

Lichen Folded Bowl | 2004

3 X 4½ X 4½ INCHES (7.6 X 11.4 X 11.4 CM)

Copper, enamel, silver foil; raised

PHOTO BY ARTIST

James Thurman

Skin | 2000

3 X 6 X 6 INCHES (7.6 X 15.2 X 15.2 CM)
Steel, fir, resin; spun, turned wood, sandblasted
PHOTOS BY ARTIST

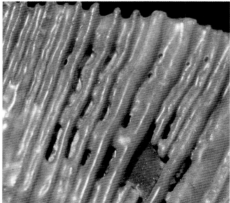

Dong Hyun Kim

Untitled Vase | 2005

9 X 6 X 6 INCHES (22.9 X 15.2 X 15.2 CM)

Copper, patina; hammered, hand fabricated

PHOTO BY MUNCH STUDIO

Cóilín O'Dubhghaill

Closed/Open Segment | 2002

LEFT, 7 X 8 X 8 INCHES (17.8 X 20.3 X 20.3 CM)
RIGHT, 2 ½ X 12 X 12 INCHES (6.4 X 30.5 X 30.5 CM)

Copper, Niiro patina; hammered, welded

PHOTO BY ARTIST

Dale Wedig

Untitled | 2003

8 X 18 X 18 INCHES (20.3 X 45.7 X 45.7 CM)

Copper; raised

PHOTO BY EDDIE PIESZCHALA

Brigid O'Hanrahan

Untitled | 1991

4 X 6½ X 6½ INCHES (10.2 X 16.5 X 16.5 CM)

Copper, silver; angle raised, constructed, soldered

PHOTO BY ARTIST

Elliott Pujol

Tuscan Vessel | 1996

5½ X 11½ INCHES (14 X 29.2 CM)

Copper, 23-karat gold

PHOTO BY PHOTOGRAPHICS
COLLECTION OF BARBARA T. PUJOL

Valentin Yotkov

Vase | 2000

12¼ X 5¼ INCHES (31.1 X 13.3 CM)
Copper, patina, beeswax;
raised, chased
PHOTO BY PLAMEN PETKOV

Maggie Yi-Shin Liu
Heaven/Earth (Earth) | 2002
3½ X 11½ X 11½ INCHES (8.9 X 29.2 X 29.2 CM)
Copper, patina; raised, etched
PHOTOS BY KATHLEEN BROWNE

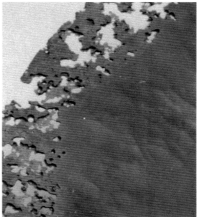

Tom Odell

Bowl | 2001

7 X 25 X 24½ INCHES (17.8 X 63.5 X 62.2 CM)

Bronze, patina; lost wax cast

PHOTO BY DEAN POWELL

Modeling in wax allows for a broad range of shaping and surface texture possibilities. Bronze was chosen for its durability and for the wide range of color possibilities available through patination. —TO

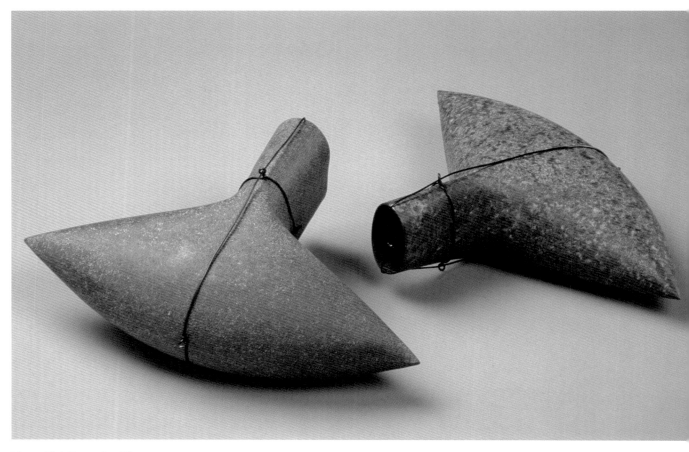

Tan-Chi Dandy Chao

Gifts | 2001

EACH, 3 X 12 X 10 INCHES (7.6 X 30.5 X 25.4 CM)

Copper, binding wire, patina; raised

PHOTO BY ARTIST

David A. Huang
Luminous Relic #496 | 2006

20 X 16 X 16 INCHES (50.8 X 40.6 X 40.6 CM)
Copper, sterling silver, 23-karat gold leaf,
patina; raised, chased, gilded

PHOTOS BY ARTIST

James Viste

Grain Bin | 2005

10 X 10 X 10 INCHES (25.4 X 25.4 X 25.4 CM)

Steel, copper, tin; forged, fabricated

PHOTO BY ARTIST

Stephen Yusko

Cross-Threaded Box | 2001

6 X 5 X 3 INCHES (15.2 X 12.7 X 7.6 CM)

Steel; forged, fabricated

PHOTO BY JEFF BRUCE

Miel-Margarita Paredes

Turkey Walker | 2005

11 X 15 X 10 INCHES (27.9 X 38.1 X 25.4 CM)

Copper, brass; raised, chased, fabricated, soldered

PHOTO BY STEPHEN FUNK

The Turkey Walker is intended for turkeys that have been bred to produce more white meat. It is from a series of "animal accessories." I have chosen animals that have been bred for a specific purpose, and the accessories I create can either facilitate or negate the purpose for which the animal is bred. Each accessory may address a perceived problem, but not necessarily the deeper issue; it is a human's interpretation of what an animal might need or want. —MMP

Marilyn da Silva

Second Nature: Sanctuary | 2006

9 X 6 X 6 INCHES (22.9 X 15.2 X 15.2 CM)

Sterling silver, copper, brass, wood, gesso, colored pencil; raised, fabricated, carved, colored

PHOTOS BY M. LEE FATHERREE
COURTESY OF MOBILIA GALLERY, CAMBRIDGE, MASSACHUSETTS

Ann E. Drewing

The Five Elements | 2006

4 X 3½ X 3½ INCHES (10.2 X 8.9 X 8.9 CM)

Copper, liver-of-sulfur patina; sunk, sawed, fold forged, acid etched, stamped, fabricated

PHOTOS BY ARTIST

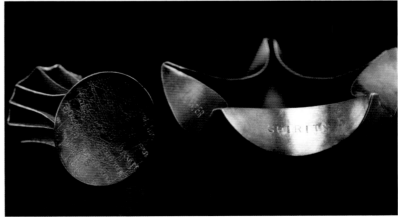

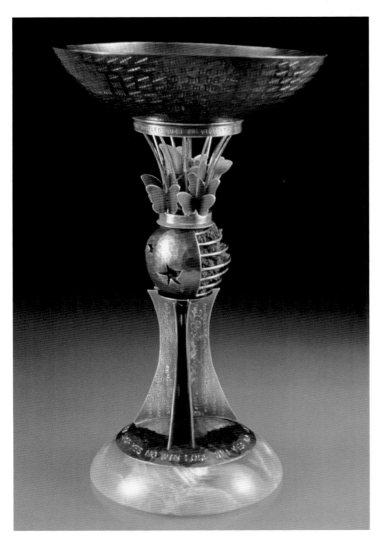

To the Spoiled *commemorates all the maddening and briefly iconic elements of the fateful 2000 U.S. presidential election process: conflicting decision announcements and endless media hype, the chads, the butterly ballots, and the constant recounts.* —NB

Nisa Blackmon

To the Spoiled Goes the Victory | 2002

9 X 5 X 5 INCHES (22.9 X 12.7 X 12.7 CM)

Copper, sterling silver, brass, model railroad vegetation, alabaster; raised, fabricated, stamped, cold connected

PHOTO BY ROB JACKSON

Lynne Hull

Totem | 1996

24 X 11 X 11 INCHES (61 X 27.9 X 27.9 CM)

Aluminum, auto body paint; spun, fabricated

PHOTO BY KEUN HATONA

Nancy Mēgan Corwin

Vase with 9 Hair Pins | 1999

15 X 3 X 3 INCHES (38.1 X 7.6 X 7.6 CM)

Sterling silver, 18-karat gold, 24-karat gold plate; hollow formed, fabricated, oxidized

PHOTO BY DOUG YAPLE

James Obermeier

Bound Vessels | 2000

LARGEST, 7½ X 8½ X 9 INCHES (19 X 21.6 X 22.9 CM)

Copper, shibuichi, shakudo, rokusho patina

PHOTO BY KEVIN MONTAGUE

Joe Muench
Hooked Vessel | 2006

10 X 6 X 6 INCHES (25.4 X 15.2 X 15.2 CM)
Steel, brass; fabricated, hand formed, textured,
hot forged, torch welded
PHOTOS BY GEORGE ENSLEY

365

James Michael Charles, Jr.

Shift | 2002

3½ X 7½ X 2¼ INCHES (8.9 X 19 X 5.7 CM)

Copper, bronze mesh, enamel, fine silver, found object;
raised, electroformed

PHOTO BY ARTIST

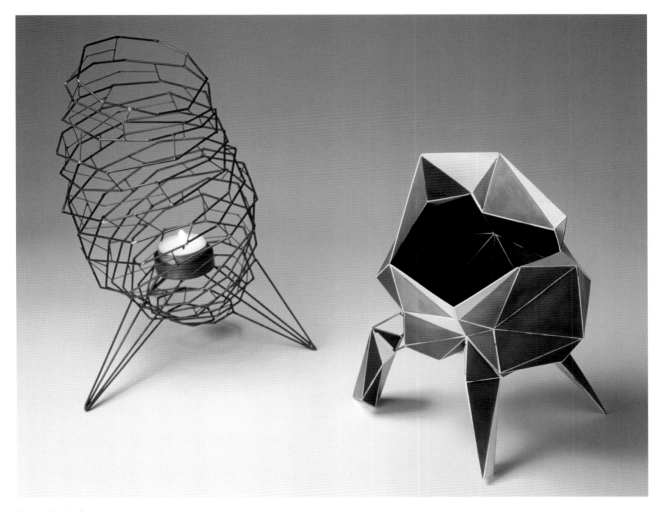

Wook Koh

Public Ownership | 2005

10½ X 7½ X 8¼ INCHES (26.7 X 19 X 21 CM)

Copper, sterling silver, steel

PHOTO BY MUNCH STUDIO

Yuh-Shyuan Chen

Vessel II | 2006

8½ X 7 X 5¼ INCHES (21.6 X 17.8 X 13.3 CM)

Aluminum; sawed, riveted

PHOTO BY ARTIST

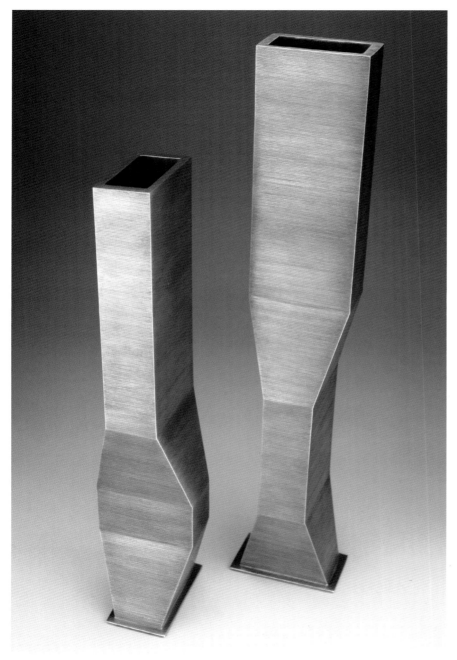

Mary McMullen

Vases | 2004

15 X 5 X 5 INCHES (38.1 X 12.7 X 12.7 CM)
12 X 5 X 5 INCHES (30.5 X 12.7 X 12.7 CM)

Pewter

PHOTO BY STEVEN FUNK

Simon Cottrell

Spilt Milk Jug | 2001

5 X 3 X 2 INCHES (12.7 X 7.6 X 5.1 CM)

Monel 400, 16-karat green gold; soldered, fabricated

PHOTOS BY ARTIST

Min Jeong Kim

Trinity | 2005

8 X 8 X 4¾ INCHES (20.3 X 20.3 X 12 CM)

Brass, graphite

PHOTO BY MUNCH STUDIO

Dennis Nahabetian

Spring Lotus | 2006

3⅝ X 10 X 10 INCHES (9.2 X 25.4 X 25.4 CM)

Copper, bronze, polychrome with cosmetics

PHOTOS BY ARTIST

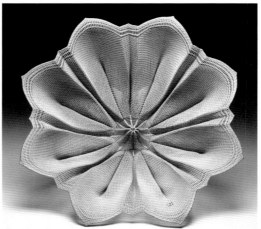

Soon Chan Hwang

Embossed | 2005

9½ X 9½ X 3 INCHES (24.1 X 24.1 X 7.6 CM)

Stainless steel, sterling silver; folded

PHOTO BY MYUNG-WOOK HUH, STUDIO MUNCH

...*A house for a host of heavenly spirits. Raise the roof and make a joyful noise!* —KK

Kristi Kloss

Jubilant Libations | 2003

5½ X 3 X 1 INCH (14 X 7.6 X 2.5 CM)

Sterling silver; embossed, photoetched, fabricated

PHOTOS BY KAREN CARTER
COLLECTION OF BRYAN PARK

Matthew Hollern with Pamela Argentieri

Life Sketches I, II, III | 1998

EACH, 11 X 7 X 3 INCHES (27.9 X 17.8 X 7.6 CM)

Pewter, graphite, enamel

PHOTO BY ARTIST
COURTESY OF SMITHSONIAN AMERICAN ART
MUSEUM'S RENWICK GALLERY, WASHINGTON, D.C.

Yeonkyung Kim

Step by Step | 2001

9 X 9 X 3 INCHES (22.9 X 22.9 X 7.6 CM)

Brass

PHOTOS BY MYUNG-WOOK HUH, STUDIO MUNCH

Ju-Wen Hsiao
Bowl. Cup-a, Bowl. Cup-b | 2003
7 ¾ X 4½ X 4½ INCHES (19.7 X 11.4 X 11.4 CM)
Bronze; Raised, soldered
PHOTOS BY TOM MC INVAILLE

Kenneth C. MacBain

Untitled Vessels | 2005

8½ X 4½ X 3 INCHES (21.6 X 11.4 X 7.6 CM)

Sterling silver, 18-karat gold, amethyst, peridot

PHOTO BY ARTIST

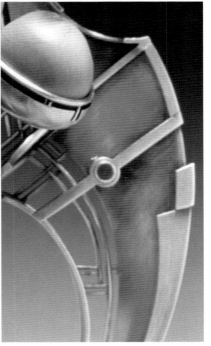

Cappy Counard

Precious | 2002

4½ X 1⅝ X 1½ INCHES (11.4 X 4.1 X 3.8 CM)

18-karat gold, sterling silver, nicker nut, springs, magnets; scored, folded, fabricated

PHOTOS BY ARTIST

Mark Herndon

Space Vessel #5 or Canaveral | 2004

6 X 5 X 5 INCHES (15.2 X 12.7 X 12.7 CM)

Damascus steel, brass, copper

PHOTOS BY ARTIST

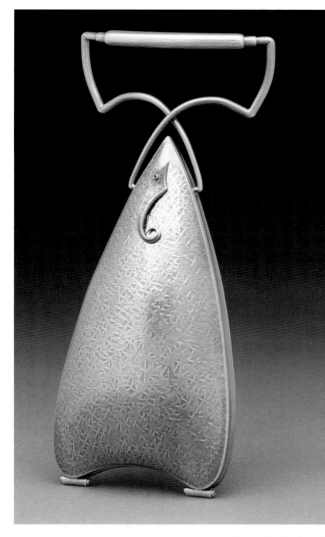

This handbag houses three implements that screw into a main neckpiece. It is based on the superficial things people do to attract others. The piece appeals to the sense of touch, sight, and smell. —AB

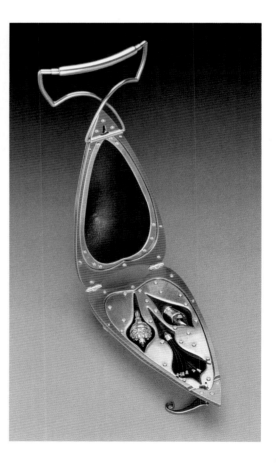

Angela Bubash

Implements for Enticement | 2003–2004

7 X 2½ X 1½ INCHES (17.8 X 6.4 X 3.8 CM)

Sterling silver, copper, stainless steel, glass, leather, rubber, garments, diamiana, vetiver, jasmine, straw flower; forged, fabricated, die formed, cast

PHOTOS BY TOM MILLS

Renée Zettle-Sterling

Study in the Ephemeral #3 | 2005

5¾ X 3 X 1½ INCHES (14.6 X 7.6 X 3.8 CM)

Copper, silver, bubble solution, air

PHOTO BY DAVID SMITH

Noël Yovovich

Late in the Day | 2006

6 X 5 X 3 INCHES (15.2 X 12.7 X 7.6 CM)

Sterling silver, copper, brass, titanium, black coral, onyx;
etched, constructed

PHOTOS BY LARRY SANDERS

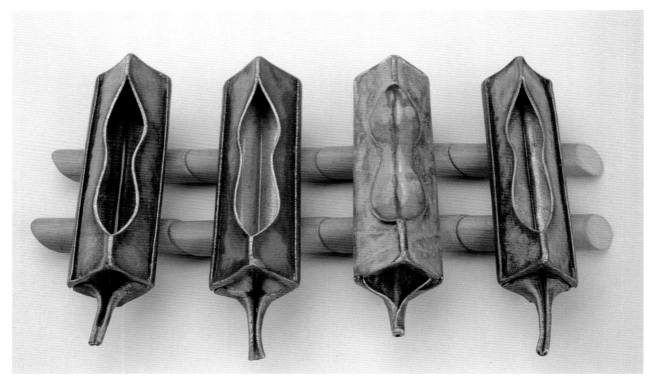

Deborah Lozier

From Mother to Son, Father to Daughter | 2004

EACH, 4³/₈ X 1 X 1 INCH (11.1 X 2.5 X 2.5 CM)

Enamel, copper, wood; fabricated, etched

PHOTO BY ARTIST

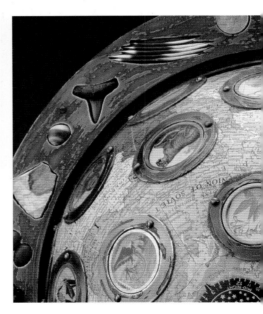

Chris Ramsay

Endangered | 2001

15 X 12 X 11 INCHES (38.1 X 30.5 X 27.9 CM)

Bronze, steel, globe, postage stamps, resin, found objects

PHOTOS BY DON WHEELER

Darlys Ewoldt

View from Above | 2003

10 X 24 X 23 INCHES (25.4 X 61 X 58.4 CM)

Copper, patina; angle raised, formed, fabricated

PHOTO BY ARTIST

Helen Shirk

Commemorative Cup | 2000

12 X 31 X 10 INCHES (30.5 X 78.7 X 25.4 CM)

Copper, patina, colored pencil; formed, fabricated

PHOTOS BY ARTIST

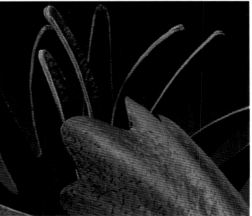

Alisha Marie Boyd

Untitled | 2006

12 X 3¾ X 3 INCHES (30.5 X 9.5 X 7.6 CM)

Copper, enamel; forged, sifted

PHOTOS BY ARTIST

Among the most primal of vessels, the spoon certainly has revolutionized the ability of humans to feed themselves. —SB

Shellie Bender

Fred and Ginger | 2003

EACH, 4½ X 1¼ X ¾ INCH (11.4 X 3.2 X 1.9 CM)

18-karat gold, sterling silver, sardonyx, ocean jasper, malachite, jade; fabricated, roll printed

PHOTO BY KENT VAN HOESEN

Nancy Slagle

Red Bud Tea Server | 2001

3½ X 6 X 3 INCHES (8.9 X 15.2 X 7.6 CM)

Sterling silver, wood, paint; die formed, constructed

PHOTO BY ARTIST

Harlan W. Butt

Earth Beneath Our Feet: Texas Teapot #1 | 2006

7 X 8 X 5 INCHES (17.8 X 20.3 X 12.7 CM)

Silver, enamel; raised, cloisonné, etched, cast, fabricated

PHOTOS BY RAFAEL MOLINA

Don Porritt

A Pair of Related Flagons | 2004

TALLEST, 9¼ X 3 X 3 INCHES (23.5 X 7.6 X 7.6 CM)

Standard silver; raised, seamed, fabricated

PHOTO BY ANDRA NELKI

I'm intrigued by architecture and captivated by the meticulous detail and level of superior craftsmanship achieved in gothic cathedrals. Although the appearance of this piece is reminiscent of the gothic era, it also speaks volumes about my personal aesthetic. My wish to create interest on every surface and encourage curiosity from the viewer manifests itself as heavily embellished and textured facades. The use of ornamentation instills a sense of majesty and interest to every aspect of the piece and aids the viewers' eyes in traveling through the design. —TF

Tom Ferrero

Teapot | 2006

6 X 6 X 4½ INCHES (15.2 X 15.2 X 11.4 CM)
Sterling silver, 22-karat gold, bone; fabricated,
raised, pierced, hand stamped, carved

PHOTO BY DAN NEUBURGER

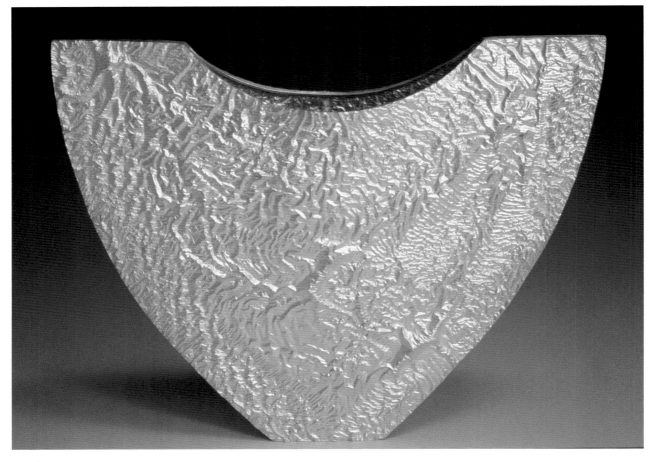

Paulette Myers

Spirit Shield | 2003

8½ X 10 X 3 INCHES (21.6 X 25.4 X 7.6 CM)

Sterling silver; fabricated, reticulated

PHOTO BY ARTIST

Susan Karesh Coddon

Ikebana Inclined Teapot | 2006

12¼ X 12 X 3¾ INCHES (31.1 X 30.5 X 9.5 CM)

Sterling silver, 22-karat gold, fossilized Alaskan tree-form coral; forged, planished, hand formed, hammer textured, mizzy-wheel textured

PHOTO BY BART KASTEN AND HELEN BLYTHE-HART

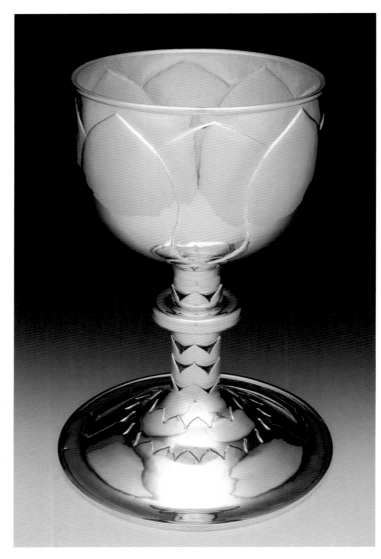

Christopher A. Hentz

Untitled | 1998

10 X 6 X 6 INCHES (25.4 X 15.2 X 15.2 CM)

Sterling silver; raised, repoussé, fabricated

PHOTO BY RALPH GABRINER

David Damkoehler

Kiddush Cup with Cover | 1998

10 X 3 INCHES (25.4 X 7.6 CM)

Stainless steel; tig welded, cold forged, lathe turned

PHOTOS BY MICHAEL MAU

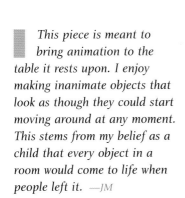

This piece is meant to bring animation to the table it rests upon. I enjoy making inanimate objects that look as though they could start moving around at any moment. This stems from my belief as a child that every object in a room would come to life when people left it. —JM

Jesse Mathes

Happy Teapot | 2001

8½ X 7 X 3½ INCHES (21.6 X 17.8 X 8.9 CM)

Sterling silver, acrylic; raised, fabricated, carved, dyed

PHOTO BY HELEN SHIRK

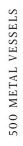

Tom Muir

Espresso Server | 2000

11½ X 2¾ X 5 INCHES (29.2 X 7 X 12.7 CM)

Sterling silver, aluminum, acetal; formed, fabricated, chased

PHOTOS BY TIM THAYER

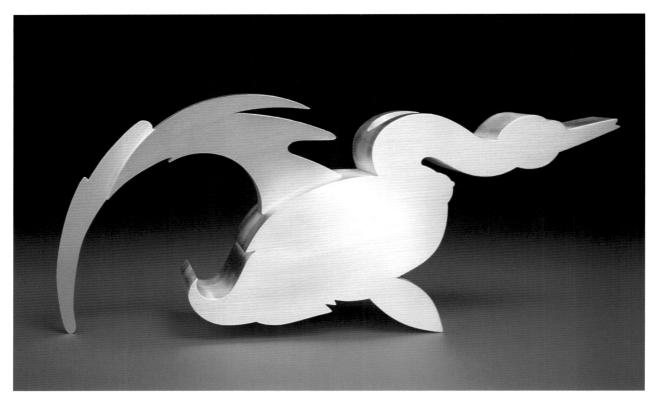

Robly A. Glover

Leda | 2002

5 ½ X 12 ½ X 2 ¾ INCHES (14 X 31.8 X 7 CM)

Sterling silver; constructed

PHOTO BY ARTIST
COURTESY OF VICTORIA AND ALBERT MUSEUM, LONDON, ENGLAND

David Bausman

Airavata | 2006

8 X 9 X 3 INCHES (20.3 X 22.9 X 7.6 CM)
Sterling silver; die formed, sheet
constructed, fabricated

PHOTOS BY ARTIST

Contributing Artists

Aalund, Nanz
Waukesha, Wisconsin
Page 204, 279

Ackelmire, Corey
Cuyahoga Falls, Ohio
Page 309

Alter, Molly Groom
Murphysboro, Illinois
Page 302

Amendolara, Suzanne
Edinboro, Pennsylvania
Page 10, 228

An, Eun-Kyung
Seoul, South Korea
Page 171

Anderson, Bruce
Stanfordville, New York
Page 120

Archibald, Alexis Rae
San Diego, California
Page 326

Argentieri, Pamela
Cleveland Heights, Ohio
Page 375

Auman, Megan
Jonestown, Pennsylvania
Page 115

Babikian, Hratch
Philadelphia, Pennsylvania
Page 147, 195

Bailey, Amy
San Jose, California
Page 23

Bally, Boris
Providence, Rhode Island
Page 35, 157, 168

Banner, Michael and Maureen
Monterey, Massachusetts
Page 51

Barnes, Nick Grant
Silver Spring, Maryland
Page 78

Bausman, David
Laredo, Texas
Page 91, 401

Bayless, Heather
Seoul, South Korea
Page 125, 293

Bayne, Barbara
Montagne, Massachusetts
Page 65, 280

Becker, Kerstin
Munich, Germany
Page 194

Bekic, Lilyana
San Diego, California
Page 237, 283

Bender, Shellie
Lawrence, Kansas
Page 389

Benzaquen, Jessica
Seattle, Washington
Page 265

Blackmon, Nisa
Champaign, Illinois
Page 361

Blair, John
Calgary, Canada
Page 203

Blyfield, Julie
Adelaide, Australia
Page 128, 269

Bostelmann, Saskia
Madrid, Spain
Page 84

Boyd, Alisha Marie
Halifax, Canada
Page 388

Brennan, Kathleen A.
Johnstown, Colorado
Page 70, 104

Bubash, Angela
Penland, North Carolina
Page 282, 381

Bush, Cody
Carenco, Louisiana
Page 134

Butt, Harlan W.
Denton, Texas
Page 159, 250, 391

Blythe-Hart, Helen
Stockbridge, Georgia
Page 207

Caro
Toronto, Canada
Page 337

Cathey, Kate
Wilmington, North Carolina
Page 133

Chader, Becky I.
Tempe, Arizona
Page 158, 314

Chao, Tan-Chi Dandy
Taipei, Taiwan
Page 188, 218, 354

Charles, Jr., James Michael
Milwaukee, Wisconsin
Page 366

Chen, Yuh-Shyuan
Tainan, Taiwan
Page 368

Cheng, Li-Sheng
Dunsden, England
Page 127

Choi, Ji-Eun
Gyeongi-Do, South Korea
Page 59

Choi, Ji Hoon
Seoul, South Korea
Page 235

Chotard, Cathy
Montpellier, France
Page 121

Chwae, Agnes
Madison, Wisconsin
Page 85, 329

About the Juror

FRED FENSTER is a distinguished artist and revered metals educator, with a passion for pewter, silversmithing, and ceremonial vessels. He was elected a Fellow of the American Crafts Council in 1995 and won the third Hans Christiaansen Memorial Silversmithing Award in 2002, the James Renwick Alliance Award in 2004, and a Gold Medal from the American Crafts Council in 2005.

Fenster's work appears in numerous public and private collections, including the Smithsonian American Art Museum's Renwick Gallery, Washington, D.C.; Milwaukee Art Museum, Milwaukee, Wisconsin; Detroit Institute of Art, Detroit, Michigan; Yale University Art Gallery, New Haven, Connecticut; Skirball Cultural Center, Los Angeles, California; and National Museum of Contemporary Art, Seoul, South Korea.

A Professor Emeritus at the University of Wisconsin, Madison, Fenster has also taught classes at Penland School of Crafts, Penland, North Carolina; Haystack Mountain School of Crafts, Deer Isle, Maine; Peters Valley Craft Center, Layton, New Jersey; and Arrowmont School of Arts & Crafts, Gatlinburg, Tennessee, as well as for other university programs.

Acknowledgments

We were incredibly fortunate to work with Fred Fenster, the juror of this book. His knowledge, passion, enthusiasm, and sense of humor made the process of selecting these vessels a delightful and enriching experience.

We are deeply appreciative of all of the metalsmiths who submitted images for this publication. Without their willingness to share their talent with Lark Books and its readers, we could never have created this book. We are consistently amazed and inspired by their imagination, innovation, and dedication to the medium.

A warm thank you to the galleries, guilds, and schools that vigorously promote and enrich the metal arts. They contributed immeasurably to disseminating information about this book and to ensuring the volume of submissions we received.

We're indebted to our first-rate editorial assistants —Mark Bloom, Brian Daignault, Dawn Dillingham, Rosemary Kast, and Sarah Nightingale. Their careful attention to detail kept the process smooth and on track. Thanks to art department assistants Shannon Yokeley, Lance Wille, and Travis Medford for their steadfast support during the book's production. Thank you to Kathy Holmes for her impeccable design; we couldn't ask for a better showcase for the vessels.

Marthe Le Van and Cassie Moore